LAINGEN ON LEADERSHIP

II

LAINGEN

ON

LEADERSHIP

II

Charles W. Laingen

Dedicated to the memory of my Mother,

Penelope Babcock Laingen,

the "Mother of the Yellow Ribbon," who led a creative,
inspired life and exemplified leadership
for family, community and country.

Contents

Preface

This collection of brief essays is the *second* of two volumes that represent my views about leadership, developed from a 21-year career in the U.S. Navy and 19 years in the business world.

When I made the transition from a Navy career to the civilian world, I was expecting a sea change when it came to the employment of leadership skills I had developed in the service. I was surprised to learn that in most ways, nothing was different. Human nature doesn't fundamentally change when one dons a uniform or hangs one up. We are all still driven by the same passions, and we respond in the same ways to calm, purposeful and inspired leadership, no matter the venue.

I've been privileged to be inspired by many great mentors in the Navy and the business world, who have shown me, through actions and words, that wherever you end up in life, *leadership matters.*

Charles W. Laingen
Woodbury, Minnesota
February 24, 2023

LAINGEN ON LEADERSHIP

II

Leadership & Teaching It

It's an age-old question: Can you teach leadership? Better stated, can you really teach people to be effective leaders? I'd answer that with a brief anecdote.

My first squadron was the "McHales's Navy" of the helicopter Navy. For those who don't know that old TV sitcom reference, it means we were the least-resourced unit in the service – an island of misfits with rotary wing toys befitting of our station. After my first pre-flight of one of the squadron's well-used H-3 Sea King aircraft, I asked the maintenance master chief, with some hesitation: *"Will it fly?"* He just shrugged his shoulders and said, *"Well, it'll get off the ground sure enough, but you'll have to do what you can to keep it there."*

Fast-forward to my academic after-life at a major university... the most respected fellow-professor in our program was Professor Kirk Froggatt, principally because of his un-matched ability to connect with students in his leadership classes. When asked about his approach to teaching leadership, he answered this way:

"I don't teach leadership knowledge. What I really try to do is be a talent developer who helps people develop confidence and capability in performing as a leader. So performance is my goal, not knowledge."

Like the master chief in my first squadron who believed that our old aircraft were capable of basic flight, Professor Froggatt knows that when it comes to effective leadership, the raw material for success is generally within most people, to varying degrees. But to really perform, leaders need guidance, mentorship and lessons from practical application, as much as old aircraft need skilled and attentive aviators at the controls. It's not helpful to simply lay out the time-tested principles of leadership and hope they get followed. The teaching has to involve building the "confidence and capability" of the individual as well. Good leadership just won't fly without that level of instruction.

Leadership & Customer Obsession

Amazon has a set of 16 "Leadership Principles" that it prominently displays during its hiring process (no, I'm not looking to be employed at my neighborhood's new fulfilment center). Right at the top is *"Customer Obsession: Leaders start with the customer and work backwards. They work vigorously to earn and keep customer trust... (and) they obsess over customers."*

A leader so exclusively focused may be tempted to create an organizational culture that resembles the scientific methods put forth by Frederick Taylor in the late 1800s: clear division of tasks and responsibility; higher pay for higher-performers; hierarchical authority; and strict surveillance of employees. Taken to its extreme, that model ultimately became criticized for its potential to de-humanize and de-moralize the workforce.

As with any extreme, along came advocacy for a wholly different approach – including with the "Hawthorne studies" in the early 1900s that suggested leadership should shift to more exclusive attention to social relationships driven by human nature, over production requirements controlled by data and customer fulfilment. If one delves into Amazon's remaining 15 Leadership Principles, one might see its more balanced approach that only at first suggests total customer obeisance.

The U.S. Military's culture reflects a similar balance between customer and employee, in their case between mission and service member. Notwithstanding the higher pay advocated by Taylor (one could substitute promotion and medals, I suppose), its culture is a lot like his cold, quantitative method; yet our same Military pulls off a surprisingly humanized culture suggested by the Hawthorne studies, as evidenced by its creation and shaping of the "diversity and inclusion" movement that our broader society later adopted; and by its model for servant leadership that much of the officer corps exemplifies.

As much as I value balance in all things (I do believe it's an immutable law of nature in all human interaction), when it comes to effective leadership it seems to set up an unnecessary tension: that one has to alternate time and attention between customer and employee; between mission and service member. I prefer to think of leadership not so much as balance between these things as *parallelism* among them. One can give equal and full treatment to both, albeit in different ways. The Secretary of the Navy in 2001 coined a phrase that one occasionally hears to this day: *"Mission First, People Always."* That's a cogent, succinct way to say that the customer obsession is the mission, but only resourced and inspired employees can satisfy that obsession... dynamics of parallel importance.

Effective leadership requires an *obsessive* desire for mission and customer excellence; and a parallel servant's dedication to those we lead.

Leadership & Five Awesome Books

This is a deviation from my normal essays about leadership, but here goes... I'm not a voracious reader, but I know people who are, and I envy them. Reading - truly reading, actual books, a LOT - is something the very best leaders do, and I find myself trying to be like them. Someday perhaps I'll get there. Nonetheless, I've done a fair bit of reading, and the following is my list of books that I believe are excellent resources for leadership development, each for different reasons.

1) The Career Manifesto (Mike Steib, 2018): This is a career reflection guide, similar to "What Color Is Your Parachute?" In my view it goes further, guiding you to consider your own leadership traits and potential. It's also a great read to recommend to those you lead and serve - a way to demonstrate to them that you're ready to consider and inspire their own leadership potential in equal measure to your own.

2) The Cruel Sea (Nicholas Monsarrat, 1951): Dated? Yes. A really niche novel about the brutal naval conflict in the great North Atlantic U-Boat theater in WWII? Yes. But this historical fiction epic is the most beautifully-written treatise on leadership in crisis ever written. Its lessons are applicable from the warship to the family to the boardroom. Read it and prove me wrong.

3) Smart Brevity (Jim VandeHei, 2022): The older I get, the more I believe that effective leadership is about communicating concisely. This brief, pithy self-help book should be mandatory reading for anyone who wants to influence people by conveying information of any kind. Its simple but ingenious methodology is pure gold for leaders who want to be heard in today's noisy arena.

4) 12 Rules for Life: An Antidote for Chaos (Jordan B. Peterson, 2018): This choice will be as controversial as is its Canadian philosopher-author. I agree with most of what he says, because he gets to the heart of the most un-changeable force of nature: human nature. Others think human nature is evolving; which is more reason to read Peterson, who doesn't. Either way, as one reviewer said: "Peterson can take the most difficult ideas and make them entertaining." Whatever one's own beliefs about human nature, effective leaders aspire to understand the nature of the humans they lead. This book will take you there.

5) An un-named book of your choice (TBD, any date): This is not a cop out. First, I didn't want to list my own book on leadership, since that's pretty self-serving; and by not listing it but mentioning it, I've just checked that block. But more importantly, this is meant as a way to recommend "stepping out of your comfort zone," as the saying goes. Pick an author that you know in your heart you would likely fundamentally disagree with for whatever reason (like the aforementioned Peterson); and make it a point to read him or her. Challenging our beliefs, and perhaps ultimately taking on at least some of the beliefs of others, is a hallmark of great leadership.

Read. Enjoy. Repeat. Lead.

Leadership & A Few Good Habits

I've written many articles about leadership, and they're likely getting redundant; but we're all human, and being an effective leader means even the best leaders need reminding. Here are 10 good habits to think about as you continue to lead – and improve.

1) <u>Listen actively</u>. Walkabouts and casual interactions can reveal a lot about your organization and the morale of those who serve in it if you truly are in "receive" mode. Ask your people questions, and be ready to receive answers you may not want to hear. And don't feel the absolute need to respond, necessarily, other than to perhaps ask more questions. The retort *"Tell me more about that"* is an effective one that I learned from a fellow educator who promotes class participation, and is admired greatly by her students. It signals real interest and validation in someone's opinion.

2) <u>Serve rather than lead</u>. You don't need to direct and supervise and order and manage *all* the time. In fact, think about doing that almost none of the time. Instead, put your time into empowering those who actually do the work. Leadership is more of an example than an action. My favorite ship's captain spent much more time finding ways to get his Sailors promoted than his ship's reputation advanced. In the end, both were accomplished *because* of the first.

3) <u>Demonstrate sacrifice, not expectation</u>. We're increasingly living in an entitlement culture, but successful organizations ultimately refute that. They build, and manufacture, and act; they don't wait for things to happen, or for recognition to come. As a result people need to be reminded that the reward must also be in the work itself, not just in the fruits of its outcomes. Your own example of that is critical to the organization.

4) <u>Don't ever say you're too busy, even if you are</u>. You are supposed to reflect calm, measured leadership that includes effective time management and prioritization. If you come across as frenetic and disorganized, so will those who follow your example. If you really are that busy, it's time to delegate and divest and purge anyway. One of my squadron commanders once said, *"If you can't manage well enough to get your ground job done, then we'll take you off the flight schedule."* That fixed that problem.

5) <u>Champion your people, not yourself</u>. This is a corollary to #2 and the principle of servant leadership. Leadership is ultimately not about you. It's about the people and the organization you lead and what they're supposed to be accomplishing. Do that by raising up your people, praising them, promoting them and caring so much about them that you genuinely hope they out-perform and outrank you some day. That's how much you should champion them.

6) <u>Mission first; people always</u>. This was a phrase that one of our Navy Secretaries came up with, to challenge our contention at the time that we should put our Sailors above all else. Not really, he said – we really exist for the mission – and that *has* to be the number one priority. But it was also a recognition that Sailors get that mission accomplished, and *"people always"* was a clever way to say that the two go hand-in-hand. Serve them, yes; but hold high standards and expect excellence from them because the mission is paramount.

7) <u>Build a culture of 'YES</u>.' I've been working a lot lately with economic development entities in North Dakota. There's a healthy and strong overlay of action-oriented leadership there that pervades everything they do, and that's noticeably different than in many other states. It didn't take long to understand what was different: everyone is pre-wired to say *'yes'* to opportunities they are presented with, no matter the level of the challenge. What a great, positive expression of leadership.

8) <u>Personify and build a culture of respect</u>. Leaders who honor everyone for their contributions, value their differences without special favor for anyone's differences, and treat everyone equally with dignity and respect likely run excellent organizations. Organizations that have "Diversity, Equity and Inclusion" programs likely only need them because they lack the genuine leadership that personify what such programs profess to teach. Training courses don't build exemplary organizational cultures – exemplary leadership does.

9) <u>Be actively grateful</u>. I learned late in life that gratitude takes work. Yes, you might be grateful now and then about things that occur, and then internalize the feeling. But working at it, being intentionally grateful, is a habit that can be improved upon as surely as physical exercise. When it becomes ingrained, and your gratitude is naturally expressed to others as a matter of instinct, your leadership skills get markedly better.

10) <u>Know your business. Know your people. Know yourself</u>. This trifecta is as old as human nature itself when it comes to effective leadership. It doesn't really need to be further explained. But it's helpful to reflect on people you've known in your own life who you respect as great leaders. I'll guarantee they've exemplified all three. Look to their example of how well they did that, and emulate them.

There are ten more great habits… and ten more after that… and you'll never master all of the traits that make great leaders. But you can master the practice of working on those habits, a little bit each day. Those you lead and serve will be glad you did.

Leadership in Business & The Perfect Autorotation

When life gets challenging, people tend to fall back on what they know, and rely on the tools they grew up with. For me, that past history was aviation – specifically helicopter aviation. A challenging day was when the engine quit, and we were forced to enter an "autorotation" (essentially the craft's version of a powerless airplane gliding to a hopefully successful landing). There are a lot of things to deal with simultaneously during an autorotation and the successful management of all of them is required for a smooth touchdown (aka survival).

In my second life, I've seen a lot of companies have engine failures – caused by sudden market changes (sudden competition and a pandemic to name just two) – and have to enter an autorotation, with the hope of a successful landing. As with a helicopter, the complexities can be overwhelming. Paying attention to all of them *simultaneously* is critical; hence another reason why truly effective leadership is so challenging. As the helicopter's engine winds down, it's no different for a business that has to adapt to sudden change or not survive. To help in that difficult process, here's a helicopter autorotation checklist, and its business equivalent:

1. Put the collective down (take power out to ensure that you maintain rotor speed): In other words, make the decision to change the business. Without this decisive initial leadership decision, the craft is doomed, and quickly. Act now, as the market dictates a new direction.

2. Apply right rudder pedal (counteract the torque change that putting the collective down caused). In business, make immediate adjustments to the forced correction as required, whether it's tooling up for a new product line, or engaging HR to get the right hires in place. As with torque, for every action

you take in business there's generally an equal and opposite reaction. Being ready for it is fundamental to success.

3. <u>Move the throttle to idle</u> (ensure power is off the rotor system – at least until full engine power is restored). This is the "grace period" in business. Pause for a time, given your sudden change, and analyze your new direction. Consult with the board, get feedback from your employees and most importantly your customers. Things move quickly, but not so quickly that you can't analyze the corrections you've made and ensure they're on track (as you plummet toward the ground).

4. <u>Turn to the right heading for landing</u> (the aircraft needs a safe landing spot, into the wind if possible). You're committed now, to a new path for the company, with some minor corrections during your brief control corrections and idle period. Start to define what your perfect landing site and its parameters look like, so that you're more prepared once you get there.

In helicopter aviation, these four critical steps are the *"Down, Right, Idle, Turn"* portion of the autorotation. The immediacy is now on hold for a brief time, as you've handled the emergency and committed to your new fate during a glide period. Now it's time to manage the business of flying a new, interim mission – the fine tuning to set yourself up for the perfect landing. It's time to monitor some things like:

- <u>Airspeed</u>: are your employees going at the same rate as you toward the destination? Are you communicating regularly and at a pace that they can keep up with the change?
- <u>Attitude</u>: in a helicopter, it's the right level of the nose on the horizon to ensure the correct airspeed and heading. In business, it's ensuring that you're getting

your employees the resources and training they need to achieve the expected landing.

- <u>Ball</u>: in the aircraft this means balanced flight, which is crucial to ensure the right rate of descent and control inputs. In business, you'll need to achieve *balance* too – both the change that's occurring <u>and</u> the natural resistance to it.

Finally, it's time to land firmly but safely, ready for a new takeoff that the market has dictated to you. In aviation, an autorotation is admittedly fairly prescriptive. In business, it's less easy, as you're dealing with far more variables that come from human nature – something that a helicopter thankfully doesn't have… except perhaps a French helicopter (but that's the subject of a different article).

As you land at a new place in business, you're hopefully on a better trajectory for the new mission. But because of the aforementioned human nature, there will be some changes, and even losses that have occurred along the way. Not everyone will have followed you on the new path, and the business will now have new dynamics to deal with. Your H-3 is now an H-60… more expensive and more complex probably; but inherently more capable. It's now time to re-fuel and launch the business to new airspeeds and altitudes.

If you've been willing to follow this admittedly torturous analogy thus far, you deserve an Air Medal, or a Business Excellence Medal. Bottom line? Effective business leadership will sometimes require a drastic correction to a sudden change, mid-flight. Your ability to manage a lot of change simultaneously, while remaining committed to an unexpected destination, could mean keeping the company viable – and hopefully making it soar. Keep your eye on the many gauges and remain committed to the new landing. It will be smooth if you lead it in a decisive but balanced way. Down, Right, Idle Turn.

Leadership & Leading Before the Crisis

By now most everyone is aware of the brave and inspirational words and deeds of Ukraine president Volodymyr Zelensky following the Russian invasion of his country. He has stood brazenly in his office while praising his citizens' valor; and shown us humble, impulsive gestures like grabbing a folding chair and sitting at eye level with reporters, instead of standing behind an officious podium.

Few of us had any idea who Zelensky was in 2019, or even where Ukraine was on a map. Yet now he is not just his nation's leader, but a global icon, and a model for inspirational, servant leadership and indefatigable courage in time of extreme crisis. Yet it is this statement from his inauguration speech in 2019 that is especially revealing about the power and authenticity of his leadership:

"I don't want my portraits to hang in your offices, because the president is not an icon or an idol. Hang pictures of your children there and look them in the eyes before every decision."

These words showcase that Zelensky's power comes not from his office, nor even from his effective reaction to crisis. Rather, it comes from many years of character development when his leadership seemed to matter much less; and yet mattered every bit as much, in everyday situations. Absent crisis, that wasn't nearly as apparent, and that's entirely the point. This president's transition from peacetime bureaucracy to wartime commander in chief was effortless and masterful because he knew that crisis is simply an amplification of needs that are fundamentally no different in peace or in war. People want to feel valued, part of a unified team and central to a vision in which they can believe. And most of all they want to feel that their leadership serves them, not the other way around.

Many years ago a wise Navy captain reminded me and my fellow midshipmen that you serve and love your shipmates first, then your ship, then your service, and then your country. If you've followed those priorities as a captain, you've likely exercised authentic leadership long before a crisis. When hardships and storms and torpedoes do inevitably arrive they appear more as management challenges to be overcome. Ultimately, that calm and competence under pressure then also serves to bolster the captain's courage and decisiveness when it's needed most.

Zelensky embodies this depth and breadth of servant leadership. Russia's Putin clearly does not. It is why Ukraine will ultimately prevail. We can all benefit from this powerful example of humility and service in our everyday interactions. Leadership matters now; not just when the ship is at risk of sinking. God bless Ukraine, and the shining example of its leadership.

Leadership & Begging Forgiveness

The *"Top Gun"* movie reprise, 36 years after the original, was worth the wait, both for sheer entertainment and for its tribute to a grand, if generally unspoken naval tradition: *sometimes it's better to beg forgiveness than to ask for permission.* In *"Top Gun: Maverick,"* Tom Cruise does various things that seem incongruous with good military order and discipline... such as throwing the aircraft procedures manual in the trash in front of his students; and "stealing" an F/A-18 after being grounded, to demonstrate the feasibility of a seemingly impossible mission.

This all seems a little "Hollywood," but there's an interesting, and largely unknown, aspect to the U.S. Military, and particularly so for the sea services of the Navy, Marine Corps and Coast Guard, that would suggest otherwise: we tend to deviate from procedures now and then, to get the mission done, particularly when the risks are high and the odds of success are low. Perhaps it's the unique environment of the "cruel sea;" or maybe it's just the inflated egos of a profession that thinks its operating environment is worthy of special adulation. Either way, a curious balance sometimes plays out, when procedures written in peacetime meet the unforeseen realities of battle or nature. The result is a manifestation of leadership that values risk assessment and moderation in equal portion with risking it all for glory and God and country.

For me, that's a pretty exciting balance to embrace, in the military or in business. For where does true success in any arena happen without significant risk? What good are estimations anchored in technological guesstimations without some wild assertions that the market will respond to a buzz that you, yourself, create? I once worked for a CEO who embraced the Top Gun mindset of the sea services. He insisted that his uniquely-manufactured electrical conductors for aviation and space travel should deviate wildly from the hundred-year norm… and that it was better to beg forgiveness than to ask for permission – from the barons who allegedly controlled those markets. Today, that CEO's "space wire" constructed from carbon nanotubes is the new standard of excellence, bringing improved capability and resilience to high performance electrical conductors, some even now flying into deep space.

Risky? Hell yes. But thank God for those who are willing to light their hair on fire and beg forgiveness, rather than ask for permission. It might get them grounded as they buzz the tower, but their example is often the effective leadership we need to succeed.

Leadership & Trusting Your Gauges

Vertigo in the aviation world is a condition wherein the pilot's sense of attitude, direction and speed contradicts the reality of the aircraft's true orientation.   It occurs most often in "Instrument Meteorological Conditions" (IMC). Put simply the pilot can't see out the windows thanks to clouds, darkness, fog or heavy precipitation which can lead to disorientation. Every pilot I know has experienced it, to some degree.   It's a disconcerting feeling, and potentially dangerous.   When it's bad, down seems up; left seems right, acceleration becomes deceleration, descent becomes climb.   Mitigating vertigo involves transferring controls to your copilot (if you have one), getting back to visual conditions, or – most commonly – relying on your gauges (instruments), notably the attitude gyro, and the airspeed and vertical speed gauges. Pilots train heavily on this latter remedy (because our egos don't lend themselves to admitting we're confused and giving up control of the aircraft or flying into "easier" conditions).

Trust me that sometimes it's really hard to rely on your gauges in IMC, particularly in heavy turbulence, or after many hours of flying, even with extensive training and experience. You're descending fast and turning sharply right, but every part of your being is saying you're doing the exact opposite. If you trust your gauges you can overcome the false signals. If you believe your brain, you can exacerbate the situation with incorrect control inputs. I've had to take controls from a more senior pilot because of this very situation (and admittedly surrender controls myself on other occasions).

Leadership of an organization can be a lot like vertigo in flight. Leaders can find themselves in the analogous IMC-like conditions of turbulent, cloudy or dark human nature, and start to make the wrong inputs based on their instincts and past history.   And perhaps leadership is even harder, though arguably less potentially deadly, at least in the near term. That's because people aren't governed by the relatively simple laws of flight (where there are only four main dynamics, after all: lift, weight, thrust and drag); but rather by the infinite and ever-changing dynamics of the human condition.

But the analogy holds, in a way: the desired outcome is straight and level flight for the aviator; and smooth continuous performance and growth of the organization for the leader. When we get caught up in the complexities of human nature, it can be a challenge to determine what's causing the lack of visibility and the turbulence outside of our leadership cockpits. The situation has become worse today, as leaders are increasingly being made to believe that human nature has changed. It hasn't of course, and never will. People will always be motivated by the immutable needs of care and comfort, purpose and direction, and the feeling of being valued for their work.

The good news is that organizations have gauges, too; things like: profit and margin, morale, employee retention, shareholder gains and customer satisfaction. And in fact actual online "dashboards" with gauges of such measures are now common in business.

As we encounter vertigo while exercising leadership, and we all do, it's useful then to follow a three step process. First, we should ignore the obfuscation of those who tell us there's more at play, and always fall back on reinforcing the fundamentals of leadership that never change and motivate human performance. Second, it's sensible to initially go with your instincts, honed by lessons learned over time as a leader. Just as an aviator senses and expertly reacts to her aircraft and its environment, you should too.

But if you've done all that, and full-on vertigo sets in nonetheless, and the complexities of human nature start to put you in a spin, it's perhaps time to go to the gauges of business; the outcomes that we ultimately seek. Your organization is operating in an environment that's as defined as the four unalterable forces of flight – profit or loss; employee retention or dissatisfaction. If you're reading *those* gauges early enough and believe what they're telling you, you can avoid a tailspin for the business. Just as in flight, your leadership skills and instincts built over time, and the gauges that are measuring actual outcomes work hand-in-hand.

Like a lot of things in life, when you get really good at something, and instinct kicks in, that's when you're susceptible to letting your guard down, and you may start failing to see the signs that used to stand out, and that got you to your level of excellence in the first place. Aviating, and leading organizations are a lot alike in that respect. When vertigo sets in, go to your best options: navigate to clearer weather, and hand the controls off from time to time to your copilot. But by all means, keep scanning the gauges of your business for the early signs that you're departing controlled flight. They're telling you a lot, and they can give you time to level the wings, see more clearly, and perform a smooth landing.

Leadership & Transcending Mediocrity

Has anyone else noticed that we are stuck living in a sort of post-pandemic malaise? Do you get the sense that the past several years has led to a slow descent into lower standards? There seems to be a reluctant acceptance of mediocrity in all things. For a time, it seemed logical to chalk it up to the realities of social distancing and remote working. But while the pandemic has moved on, it feels like much of our professional environment has not. If we were to give marks for our current state we might recall a well-known Royal Navy officer's fitness report which included the phrase: *"He sets low personal standards and then consistently fails to achieve them."*

But here's the thing: truly effective leadership has no patience for societal ills when they affect productivity and excellence, whatever their causes, real or imagined. The fundamentals for effective leaders don't change when followers begin to surrender to hardships and challenges. In fact, the fundamentals become even more relevant and their impacts more needed. When my father was called on to lead the U.S. Embassy in Iran just prior to the hostage crisis of 1979-1981, a colleague penned an op-ed in the *Foreign Service Journal* that explained his selection from among his peers. *"Bruce Laingen,"* he said, *"is the ultimate optimist. Everything he touches becomes better; and nowhere do we need that to happen more than in Tehran."* During the 444 days of the crisis that ensued, that example of optimistic leadership helped to sustain a level of professional dignity and courage that exemplified the personal example maintained by each of the 52 hostages.

Leadership in an atmosphere of resignation is hard. When the bar is lowered across the board, leading towards excellence has little incentive; and in fact it's often suppressed, as higher authorities sometimes fight the creation of unrealistic expectations when times are tough. This is often experienced by ambitious military commanders during extended periods between conflicts. But the best of the best in leadership positions persevere through the realities of unavoidable circumstances (such as pandemics and hostage crises) and exhibit the moral courage to refuse the luxury of lower standards that may naturally ensue over time.

Perhaps the ability to effectively lead to this level, under these circumstances, is unrealistic and naive. But the alternative is bleak, and that's not an option in any context. We should at least try to heed the words from another Royal Navy fitness report: *"This officer transcends mediocrity."*

Leadership & Planning for the Worst

I'm a realist by nature – someone who would very much like to be optimistic, but believes that the world often punishes optimists; and as a result, I'm a strong believer in at least planning for the very worst as a leader. My Father was, I believe, a great leader; but he was also, unlike me, an eternal optimist, which of course has its own special merits. But before he was taken hostage at the U.S. Embassy in Iran in 1979, a more realist colleague of his exercised some leadership initiative that helped his fellow captives a great deal for the first six months of their imprisonment, by doing something a pure optimist may not have considered.

Mike Howland was the assistant security chief for the U.S. Embassy in Tehran, and he was with Ambassador Bruce Laingen and the Deputy Chief of Mission Victor Tomseth, at the Iranian Foreign Ministry on the day of the embassy's takeover, ironically pleading for added security from local forces. Hearing of militants coming over the walls of the embassy just a few miles away via walkie-talkie (this was in the days before cell phones, or even pagers), Howland feared the worst, and started contingency planning at the very local level. Looking around the room in which they were waiting to see the Iranian foreign minister, he took a standard telephone and shoved it underneath a couch as a precautionary measure in case their communications were impeded for what he thought might be a few hours.

That single land line became a covert means of communications for those three hostages who were held in that very room for the next 400 of their total 444 days in captivity (separate from the other 49, held at the embassy itself). As one might expect from the line workers of any bureaucracy in any country in the world, eventually someone noticed that the foreign ministry's phone bill included significant charges for long distance phone calls to

Washington, D.C. and to other points in the U.S. (you guessed it, to family members like me) – always at around 3:00 in the morning. Suddenly the captors realized their charges were placing calls right in front of them – but not before a full six months had transpired, and lots of useful intel had been sent to officials and family by the three hostages.

The most perfectly effective leadership includes lots of traits that certainly don't ever reside within a single person; and perhaps that's why planning for the worst as a leader – or having someone on your team who does – is a pretty reasonable contingency in and of itself. Marine Corps General James Mattis once famously said: *"Be polite, be professional, but have a plan to kill everybody you meet."* Pretty simple, albeit brutal, words… but pretty good advice, in my realistic opinion.

Leadership & The Law of 150

I once asked the captain of a U.S. Navy destroyer I was assigned to how he managed to stay so happy and seemingly worry-free. After all, he commanded a vessel that made the most complex of systems look simple, was chock full of hazardous materials and dangerous weapons, had far more things broken than working, floated in typically heavy and stormy seas miles from any support, was generally recognized only when things went wrong, and was largely operated by hormone-driven, relatively inexperienced teenagers.

"Lieutenant," he said… *"Haven't you noticed? I don't have to do a damn thing around here and I get all the credit for our success!"*

The captain ran a "tight ship" of course. He exemplified so many critical leadership traits that ensured excellence, from holding high expectations to trusting his subordinates to acting as a servant leader. But more than any captain I worked with before and since, he had mastered the art of delegation; and for those of you who know the Navy culture, that's hard for many in the surface Navy to do – or for that matter in any organization, including in business.

The British anthropologist Robin Dunbar understood the need for delegation as it relates to nature. He coined *"The Rule of 150"* which suggested a *"cognitive limit to the number of people with whom one can maintain stable social relationships and thus numbers larger than this generally require more restrictive rules, laws, and enforced norms to maintain a stable, cohesive group."* It is a phenomenon that occurs in nature also, as described by the author Malcolm Gladwell in his book "The Tipping Point" – with even bees and schools of fish naturally breaking down into groups of almost exactly 150 in order to function efficiently. Humans have followed suit also from time to time, with military companies averaging that number, and the Gore company creating a new, stove-piped leadership structure every time it grew by 150 employees.

Leadership of a "large" organization (defined here as anything greater than 150 people) naturally calls for the need to somehow deconstruct the complexity that inevitably results. A Navy destroyer is a prime example, having an average of 150 Sailors; and hence its various departments that naturally flow from human bureaucratization. Just as natural, for any leader, is the innate desire to resist letting go... to let others control things... to delegate authority. But an effective leader must delegate; not their responsibility, but certainly their authority.

The very best leaders don't actually do very much at all, in my experience. Perhaps better stated, they do an awful lot of things that ultimately allow *others* to lead on their behalf: they exemplify, teach, persuade, champion, trust, commend, communicate, listen, allow, risk and most of all **serve** those who report to them. And then they delegate authority and sit back and bask in the glory.

Leadership & Attention to Detail

Effective leaders have to pay attention to a lot of different things, all the time. The more senior one gets, and the bigger the organization gets, it seems leaders back away from the "little things," and perhaps naturally and rightfully so. But like all things about leadership, there's a caveat, and a story may help to remind us that leaders should track the small stuff, too.

Late in my naval career I was standing in the outer office of our wing's commodore, waiting to meet with him. Being the type who can't just stand and wait, I started looking around the office, and noticed several boxes of printed material. They were the programs for the commodore's change of command and retirement ceremony a week hence. This was back when we had budgets for such things, and they were beautifully-rendered, multi-page, glossy and full color booklets, complete with gold cord tying the pages together. Glancing on the back, I noticed the U.S. Navy logo and the words to Anchors Aweigh... with that second word spelled *"Away."*

Nope – we want the anchor to go "aweigh," not go "away." I casually mentioned the error to the commodore's civil service executive assistant... who promptly put in a rush order, at further taxpayer expense for a corrected order, after glaring at me for my good deed that couldn't go unpunished. The commodore's ceremony the next week was flawless, and hundreds of years of naval tradition was preserved down to the last detail.

Would letting the anchors go "away" have made any difference in the end? Admittedly, probably not much at all, and it would have at least been a conversation starter for the post-reception. But while effective leaders are responsible for the obviously important things like serving the organization's people in the moment, some of the intangible things like heritage and tradition matter too, in any institution, public or private. Those things tend to be harder to pay attention to, as they lack metrics and responsible parties. But they matter, and good leaders are careful to remember that sometimes the little things are big things, and details can matter.

So when you hear aphorisms like *"Don't sweat the small stuff, and it's all small stuff,"* there's some truth to that, as you try to remain above the fray and monitor the big picture. Good leaders, however, also take the time to pay attention to details, where and when they can. Sometimes the devil resides there, and he may be weighing anchor when you don't want it gone.

Leadership & Playing the Disappointment Card

There's a card in the leadership deck that has lots of power. It's like the Death Card in a Tarot deck. Lay it out and you may as well knife a subordinate through the heart. It's the *"I'm disappointed in you"* card in a deck full of options a leader can deal. It's extraordinarily powerful; but only provided the dealer is trusted, the deck is well-shuffled, and it rarely makes an appearance.

I was medevac'd out of the Gulf War in early 1991 toward the end of my deployment there. As the officer-in-charge of a helicopter detachment aboard a strike destroyer, leaving a leadership position during wartime was hard enough. Being the "walking wounded" was even worse (a thyroid problem of all things). I was all "woe is me," as I wandered back to the U.S. through the medevac system, through Qatar, New Delhi, the Philippines and Hawaii, and eventually back to San Diego for treatment. Once there, my squadron commander unexpectedly played the death card when I reported to his office. It started with a hearty *"welcome back,"* and *"I do hope you recover, lieutenant."* That was followed by *"I'm disappointed that you never communicated with us... we've had no idea where you were for two weeks."* That was not a casual comment from a disinterested commander. It was a very real, and intentional, dagger... right through the heart.

I knew that there was no reason to respond with *"but I thought the system would let you know,"* or any other such pathetic words. I had violated a sacred principle: keep the chain of command informed, always, and about everything, "wounded" or otherwise.

Years later, I was a squadron commander, and I played the "disappointed" card with great hesitation, but with relative certainty of the effect it would have. One of my Marine Corps flight instructors had violated the course rules, that dictated where we could, and couldn't, fly, to and from the base. I recalled my own wound from years past, and reached into my Tarot deck. I didn't rant and rave, though it would have been entirely warranted. I simply said: *"Major... I thought you were better than that."*

Dagger. Right through his crimson heart.

That Marine then proceeded to become one of the very best officers in an exemplary wardroom of more than 100 flight instructors. Leadership sometimes requires reading a situation with context, finesse and judgment, and reacting to transgressions with tools that can punish, yet rehabilitate in the same moment. The "disappointed" card is sometimes that tool. Yet it can't be played without having had the right environment built up over time... an environment of trust, in which the leader has set clear expectations for excellence, and firm guidelines with regard to transgressions. When a situation is dire enough, in *any* organization military or civilian, sometimes the quiet, calm, clear-headed but brutal "disappointed" card is just the one to play.

Leadership & "Everything is Broken All the Time"

We all remember certain phrases our parents said to us, such as *"Don't make me come back there,"* or *"I was your age once, don't forget,"* or *"You don't know anything until you have kids of your own."* My own kids will likely remember me uttering: *"Everything is broken, all the time."* There's a leadership lesson in that saying, I promise.

My realization of ubiquitous brokenness came to me about halfway into my Navy career, when being at sea on an old destroyer drove home the point, every hour of every day. A warship is a floating menagerie of thousands of machines and pumps and mechanisms and computers of all kinds; complex and finicky ones at that. They're subjected to salt water, temperature extremes, spare parts made by the lowest bidder, and kids in uniform with just enough training to keep some things running and break some others. It's largely uncontrolled chaos, all the time, and those of us who've been there are amazed when something actually works when it's needed – even with the most critical and well-maintained of systems.

It's not just warships that are broken all the time. Anyone in business can relate. The supply chain never delivers what we need on time or at the right price; our communications up and down the corporate ladder are inherently lacking or garbled; we don't have the right market intelligence to verify our assumptions; the scrap rate on the manufacturing line is out of control; our customer has found a way to break what was sold as unbreakable; and our boss hasn't delivered what we need to succeed.

It's all pretty frustrating and discouraging, if one allows oneself to be immersed in it. My roommate on one Navy destroyer was the ship's chief engineer ("CHENG"), a thankless position even on a good day with a new ship in a calm sea. When asked one night during "eight o'clock reports" (the daily update by each department head to the ship's executive officer - XO), he threw up his hands in exasperation after a particularly painful day, and coined the phrase at hand – *"Everything is broken, all the time."*

The XO gave a wry smile, nodded knowingly, and replied in a soothing voice: *"Yes, CHENG… and yet we sail on."*

That response, I thought at the time, was a beacon of hope in a stormy sea. All of the other department heads had bad news to deliver also, but their ensuing delivery had a new-found air of lightness to it, at least for one evening among many on that voyage. To be sure, things still broke on that ship, all the time, including its embarked helicopter that I was responsible for maintaining. But the XO's words were a simple gesture of calm and reassuring leadership that signaled a reason for hope, not just to the CHENG, but to all of his fellow department heads, myself included. It was also his way of reflecting empathy to a distraught colleague (he'd been a chief engineer once, too), and reminding all of us that the ship had to sail on, that we needed to still fix what we could, and to achieve the mission.

Unrelenting brokenness and the chaos it brings is why Sailors swear a lot, and with aplomb. But if you listen carefully, and for long enough, you'll perceive the truth in another phrase: *"A bitchin' Sailor is a happy Sailor."* That's because it also reveals, to the knowing, an underlying pride that comes with the chaos; that sense of achieving great things despite feeling alone and unappreciated on a relatively unsupported ship in the middle of a vast ocean.

It's remarkable how leadership can sometimes be delivered so powerfully and yet so simply – with an understanding glace, a reassuring comment, a call to stay calm and Sailor on.

Leadership & Happiness

The prolific British writer Samuel Johnson once said: *"Being in a ship is like being in jail with a chance of being drowned."* This wasn't quite my experience in the Navy, but floating about in the vast expanse of the Pacific Ocean for months on end often made one wonder. In fact one of my own Sailors once asked: *"What the hell are we doing out here, Sir?"*

It was jarring to hear the question; not because it was on most of our minds, but because one of my own Sailors asked it of me. I'd have preferred to hear just about any other question. My response in the moment, as a young lieutenant, was characteristically sarcastic to be honest, but it had me reflecting for the balance of the day about what inspired those in my 18-person aviation detachment. Another quote then came to mind, one attributed to dozens throughout history: *"The rules for happiness are: someone to love, something to do, something to hope for."*

Now admittedly I don't think employee "happiness" should be a goal of effective leadership, per se. But let's equate happiness with fulfilment at least. Having those who perform the mission *fulfilled* seems like a worthy aspiration. With that in mind, I thought of my Sailors in that triumvirate goal set. Certainly they had something herculean to *do*: maintaining a $32 Million aircraft in a salt water environment with limited tools and spare parts, not to mention working on their own qualifications for advancement. And clearly they had something to *hope for*: advancement in rate and pay, the next port visit, or the end of the deployment and a return to their loved ones.

That left "someone to love." That's a little more tricky, and I'll forego inclusion of their significant others back home, and especially the aforementioned port visits in this context. Providing them someone to love was not part of my officer's commission as far as I knew. But I could certainly provide them with some *thing* to love – and by that I mean the mission itself. The mission was our sole purpose for floating around and occasionally flying around, after all. Thinking deeper on that, I returned to my wayward Sailor's original question – "what" are we doing out here? – and provided an internal translation of sorts. That is, the real question he was asking was: *"why"* are we here?

'Why' questions are always harder to answer than 'what' questions, in my experience. But answer them well, and you can make real impact on people and their contribution to the mission. The biggest answers need to be given by higher authority, generally; in our case from the Commander-In-Chief himself and down the chain of command: national security, American presence abroad, securing the sea lines of communication, strengthening allied partnerships and all of that. Heady stuff, and supremely important, but not something the average Sailor or even officer could relate to on a day-to-day basis. So in the same vein as 'all politics is local,' what was our unit's contribution to the greater good? What we did *was* integral to it, from providing anti-submarine patrols to conducting search and rescue to bringing spare parts aboard, and a lot of other missions in between.

After such reflection, my focus at that point of the deployment became a lot more about connecting often simple, daily routines to the impact they were having on those loftier missions. This was done in myriad ways, from giving more frequent and public kudos to individual Sailors for their efforts, to casual discussions in the hangar bay or the maintenance shop about *why* the ship was performing its various missions from day to day.

Bottom line for effective leaders: look for ways to make those you lead fulfilled by the work they are doing because of the positive impact they are having on important things. Who knows, it might even make them happy, too.

Our Brit Samuel Johnson also said: *"My congratulations to you, sir. Your manuscript is both good and original; but the part that is good is not original, and the part that is original is not good."* Hopefully you can be someone who convinces those you lead that they are both good and original parts of meaningful endeavors in their lives.

Leadership & Imposter Syndrome

Albert Einstein said that *"The exaggerated esteem in which my lifework is held makes me very ill at ease. I feel compelled to think of myself as an involuntary swindler."*

And Maya Angelou is quoted as saying *"I have written 11 books but each time I think 'Uh-oh, they're going to find out now. I've run a game on everybody, and they're going to find me out.'"*

Anyone in a position of leadership or great responsibility has had similar thoughts – yes, even the most qualified in their fields. Imposter syndrome is real and ubiquitous. But what's written about it seems to always focus on the individual and the self-efficacy one can take to mitigate such feelings of being unqualified, unworthy, and ultimately found out. As leaders we often focus on our own qualities and qualifications, and we work to be more qualified and capable of our positions. That's admirable and necessary, of course.

A fellow professor provided a poignant reminder for me recently, however, that we often forget those around us have self-doubts as well. During a class discussion about effective networking in a room of eminently qualified people in their field, she told a graduate student *"Remember that you have every right to be there, too… just as much as anyone else in the room."*

Effective leadership means ensuring continuous self-improvement. But it also involves building up those you lead and convincing them that in fact they too have earned the right to be there. This is a unique element of servant leadership – being keenly aware of peoples' confidence and self-esteem. That can be hard to perceive, and only comes with true, authentic attentiveness to personas over time. It deserves the same amount of effort as the focus on the mission and its outcomes.

And if you still have doubts about your own qualifications in the meantime? Then perhaps you can channel my first instructor in flight school who told me to *"Just do like I've done... pretend like you can actually fly these expensive things and Uncle Sam will continue to let you play with them."* He also told me that we can teach monkeys to fly helicopters given enough time; so I'm not sure what that means for my own self-esteem.

Leadership & Keeping It Simple

During my time in the Pentagon I spent a week as a "loaner" officer to the Joint Staff's situation room while my own principal was on leave. It was an eye-opener in one respect; that being the crazy stuff going on in the world (trust me, you don't ever want to get a security clearance); but it was also a snooze-fest in *most* respects. Briefings consisted of tedious PowerPoints that tried to explain the unexplainable through complexity.

One morning a mere three-star general walked into the situation room to take the Chairman's briefing who was off on other duties, presumably. It's important to note that he was a Marine... officers who eschew obfuscation. The briefing officer – not a Marine – cued up his presentation, and he'd made the mistake of using a numbering convention on each slide that revealed the total number of slides. Slide one had "1 of 152" displayed in the lower right-hand corner.

The observant general looked at his watch, calmly put down his coffee, and said: *"Colonel, I trust that your 152 slides are full of wonderful information. But humor me, and advance to number 151 and tell me why I'm here and what you need from me, in five minutes or less."*

Done and done.

I frankly didn't really care about the briefing or its outcome. I'd already learned that everything in the Pentagon was important, always. Rather, as a speechwriter at the time, my thoughts turned to how I could take this lesson and turn it into a future speech theme for my own senior Pentagon official at a later date. Back in my office an hour later, I immediately used the pre-Google version of Google to search "simplicity" (yes, the U.S. Military generally has everything first). Here's likely what I got at the time:

- Life is really simple, but we insist on making it complicated. (Confucius)
- Simplicity is the ultimate sophistication. (Clare Boothe Luce)
- Wise is the one who learns to dumb it down. (Curtis Tyrone Jones)
- If you can't explain it simply, you don't understand it well enough (Albert Einstein)

It occurred to me then that truly effective leadership is not about deciphering the data in a spreadsheet. It's about absorbing that data only long enough to be decisive enough to communicate action to achieve the mission. We often get lost in the data in our time, especially now that Google is a thing. We now have the ability to analyze ad infinitum, until our own reflection becomes all that we see. The Persian philosopher *Rumi* once said: *"Look at the moon in the sky, not the one in the lake."* In other words, the reality is already there in plain sight, and it's waiting on us to react to it, not the information that put it there.

How does this relate to leadership? People certainly want to understand the mission, and to know their part in achieving it. They want to know the 'why' behind the decisions. But even more, especially if trust is in place, they want to get to work, to act, to achieve the mission. Effective leaders build a solid "appendix." That's where the data resides, in the 152-page presentations and the spreadsheets that feed them. But more importantly, they have a great executive summary that is an inspired, informed call to action.

Leadership & the "Least" Among Us

One of the greatest leaders I knew while in the Naval Service was someone who had never served in the Navy; at least not in uniform. He was, rather, the highest ranking person in the service, as Secretary of the Navy (SECNAV). I recall thinking at the time that this civilian political appointee would surely be lacking leadership skills as I understood them. I was wrong of course, and to this day I am grateful for his example on its merits, and as a reminder that truly excellent leadership can be forged by just about *any* set of life experiences.

This SECNAV exhibited his effective leadership in countless ways, from giving away credit for astounding ideas, to demonstrating how active listening could generate the best advice and counsel. But far and away his most common habit would be engaging those I'll call, for now, the "least" among us. During a visit to an aircraft carrier with 5,000-plus people, SECNAV would speak more to the most junior Sailor who had just reported aboard the ship, rather than to the captain; prior to a budget hearing before Congress he would engage with the warfighters affected by budget increases or cuts more than the officers who managed those budgets; and at black tie galas he would speak to the spouses of deployed Sailors more than to the assorted VIPs at his head table.

This all crystalized for me on the evening that the SECNAV invited his personal staff and our families to his home in Washington, D.C. during the Holidays. I recall how gratified I was that he would do so; and then how disappointed I was, initially, that he didn't spend a second with me or my colleagues during that evening. Instead, he played with our kids the entire time... and I mean *played*... on his hands and knees with Legos, doing dives with them in the pool, and showing them magic tricks in his personal study. He learned their names and looked in their eyes and said a warm goodbye to them as we left, barely acknowledging the parents as we went out the door. He was genuinely enthralled with our kids, and quite literally forgot we were even there.

It struck me then, that in fact the "least" among us were anything but. They were *everything* among us – the most junior Sailor, the spouse missing her deployed aviator, the kids for whom we were fighting to secure a peaceful future. On that special evening at SECNAV's home, my visions of sharing a bourbon with him in his private den talking world politics were replaced with admiration for a leader who had perspective for what *really* mattered. This was an example of leadership I hadn't seen before, and one that I now admired from someone in a suit every bit as much as from someone in a uniform.

It was an unforgettable lesson for me: that ultimately there really aren't "least" and "best" among us; but only "us" and one fight on our collective behalf.

Leadership & Legacy

On a recent flight I decided to change my routine, but with nothing in mind except to let something new enter it... after pouring a bourbon, of course (some routines are worth holding on to). I closed the WiFi connection, my laptop and the monitor on the headrest in front of me. The last thing I saw on the screen before closing my eyes was a random close-captioned word: *"legacy."*

That got me thinking about the great leaders I've been privileged to know in my life, and the legacy they left behind, with me and with others. I started to list them in my head, along with the different but powerful impacts they had on me...

A ship captain who found joy in every interaction he had with everyone, regardless of their rank, their role, or even their motivations for being there. He cared deeply for what they brought to the team and wanted to know, by literally asking them, what he could do to enhance both their contribution and their own satisfaction in doing so.

The corporate CEO who looked for every opportunity to connect his outwardly mundane yet highly innovative products to the higher purpose they ultimately served – that of contributing to saving lives and enhancing effectiveness for critical missions – and making sure his employees knew it and believed it.

A father who exuded courage and humility and grace in the face of extreme adversity; always putting the welfare of others before himself, even when – *especially* when – he was in the most potential peril himself.

The fellow professor who relentlessly harangued his graduate students to take their capstone projects to the next level, and to brag about themselves for their achievements along the way: *"You are amazing,"* he would say. *"Your work is amazing. Always be the amazing person that you are!"*

The unit commander who exuded the principle that leadership was not about ordering outcomes but influencing the potential for good ones; who exemplified the power of leadership by example and by storytelling, rather than by edict.

There are many more, in my experience, as well as those whose negative examples provided some clarity about what *doesn't* leave a legacy worth repeating (perhaps the subject of a future essay). What stood out for me as I looked for commonality among the very best leaders was that none of them set out to have a legacy of their own. They truly wanted those they led to have their own legacies of greatness. It's an inherent, and generally unaware selflessness that seems to be common in their natures. That of course begs the question: what if I fear that it's not in my nature to be selfless?

The answer in part is that it's not in *anyone's* nature to be completely selfless. You have to work at it, while being honest about human nature. And a good place to start after that realization is with a habit that I noticed in all of the legacy leaders from my experience. They all spent less time ordering and much more time asking, and acting on, the answers to questions like: What do you need? How can I help? What can I do for you?

The rest of the answer is that a legacy is about the future, because of what's been built in the past. You can't really control the future or the past; so it's best to focus on the here and now; and more importantly, on those whom you are leading and serving now.

(U.S.) Leadership & (Not) Maintaining a Low Profile Abroad

Prior to 9/11 I was the speechwriter to two Secretaries of the U.S. Navy (acronymically dubbed SECNAV). One spring the five of us on his personal military staff traveled to Europe ostensibly on official business, which amounted to showing the flag and collecting gifts from designated representatives of heads of states of various nations. On a three-day visit to Rome, we found that the Italians were standouts in Europe as true protocol junkies, and as a result the ride from the airport to the embassy was one for the books. It mattered not to the Italians that the civilian SECNAV was neither a cabinet level official, nor in Rome for anything terribly important. The occasion provides a glimpse into how not to manifest U.S. leadership abroad, post 9/11.

It was a scene worthy of the adjective ridiculous by any measure, whether or not one understood the happenstance by which such a scene could come about, at the historic fountain of Trevi. Amongst the gray-white, pigeon-stained and armless marble of Rome's staring Gods (themselves dumbfounded by history's charmless dismissal of their greatness some centuries previous), the traveling party of the Secretary of the United States Navy – together in august company of the Secretary and his wife themselves – *raced* through the streets in a collection of motorbikes, American vintage Dodge Ram Vans (white, stock, hubcaps, vinyl seats sans seatbelts) and a single Fiat limousine.

Raced. It was not enough that the political leader of the strongest navy 'the world has ever known' (a descriptive end-tag that the Secretary's speechwriter penned in agony when it was called for by his senior charge) had to move to his destination, from *il aeroporto* without delay. One would expect not to keep this pensive man-being in an expectant mood at any time. SECNAV's personal aide would often say that "*To idle is to invite stray thoughts, and worse – ideas. Bad. Very bad.*" No, that would not do; it was not even enough that the SECNAV had to get there post-haste. He had to get there well before that. If the motorcade was ahead of the published itinerary time, then the itinerary itself must have clearly lagged, and was thereby flawed.

The Carbinieri-cade (a reference to the sub-machine gun-toting, jack-booted motorcycle death squad that led the entourage) attacked the offending streets at a pace that kept the screaming, shaft-driven motorbikes (moto-guzzis – very fast) airborne most of the time, as they skipped off cobblestones, Roman cart tracks and the odd, unfortunate pedestrian who lay down in the path to assuage the angst of the gods, who in their marble bas-relief began to take on recognizable astonishment in their frozen gaze.

It was not that the SECNAV (Caesar) was going anywhere in particular, other than to his waiting suite at the U.S. Embassy. This was an extraneous fact which had escaped the attention of the dozens of protocol officers and lackeys who had arranged for this quasi-military mission. For it was just that – a mission: get the most important naval figurehead in the world of two-thirds water to his temporary place of residence *now,* and do it with a determination that demanded speed, ambition, crass attention-getting and death-defying motorcycle stunts, causing chaos in Carthage.

All of this produced in the traveling party an odd mix of emotions. Never mind the 'principal' and 'the Mrs.' ensconced in the 'hard car' – a black, leather-stitched coach from the best of Fiat motorwerks. An air of calm pervaded the air-conditioned interior, the stillness of which was broken only by the occasional faintly-heard screams of innocent, law-abiding citizenry, thwacked or jackbooted by the charging Carabinieri out in front, and the rustling of the New York Times Style section. Any real emotion lay within 'dash two' and 'dash three' of the motorcade, the American van-beasts containing the various charges of the big guy – now Aide, now Public Affairs Officer, now Speechwriter, and Photographer… on Dancer and Prancer… now up on two wheels to match their procession's leaders, rounding a curve as a chariot in danger of losing to a whip-wielding gladiator.

But the emotions within the following chariots were not as strong as one might imagine, save for the occasional burst of shock, dismay, horror and fear, as Detroit-forged fenders ripped and peeled open rows of Alfa Romeos, parked Italian style, akimbo and three ways on two way streets. Rather, and more prevalently, the thoughts of the traveling staff were a vague glee, a *"How 'bout this?"* and *"Oh,* much *faster than the escorts in London,"* and an urge to reminisce and wonder about how one's successful career as a helicopter pilot, combat photographer or leader of Marines might end as a crumpled mass of navy-white steel, and the red, white and blue pride of American world dominance… 'from the sea.' And all of this with an air of back-of-the-mind amusement of *"look Ma, no seatbelts!"*

A sudden roundabout, in classic Italian lane-less style, presented the motorcade with the ultimate test of centripetal force, as steering wheels were slung side to side to circulate the path as well as to cut off fellow circle-travelers. All was well momentarily, followed by the unlatched rear van doors of 'dash three' flinging themselves open to discharge the staff luggage amidst the circulating traffic. Screeching tires jarred loose ancient cobblestones and halted the Dodge, mid-circle, dislodging the staff, aka former warriors, to gather not just valises, but their contents – including formerly crisp, naval dress white uniforms and – cringingly – Mrs. SECNAV's formal dresses and unmentionables. Said garments and their retrieval were all carefully guarded by two dismounted Carabinieri, Uzis in one hand, and miniature stop-signs-on-a-stick in the other. Truly, stop-signs-on-a-stick.

Two-toned, despondent and mind-numbing sirens now emanated from the detached portion of the motorcade, to signal that the re-joining was to occur, linking again the SECNAV with his critical staff members, ensuring that the supreme, haloed, naval commander could function once again, upon his imminent arrival.

And presently King Neptune did indeed arrive, and suddenly stopped – at Trevi Fountain... not at his destination and temporary place of residence as the marble-chipped and word processor addenda'd schedule said He should be, but at Trevi Fountain. Radios crackled, pigeons flocked as visigothic rats, gypsies gathered and the Big Guy emerged from his chariot onto the crowded square, noticed at first, target-like, only by the aforementioned airborne rats.

Why, pondered the entourage, had Caesar chosen this locale to suddenly delay an already too-delayed schedule? Something naval, perchance, this way comes? Nay, something banal; something had entered the cranium of SECNAV; that knowing the tradition of coinage in fountainry, and its connection with the harkening of luck and the certitude of the thrower returning to this formerly idyllic spot had in fact originated here, at Trevi (and elsewhere, but bear no mind). Given that, a certain delay was warranted to bring good fortune to the greatest fleet the world has ever known.

Now a mere mortal tourist would produce a coin, or perhaps a metro token, from the bottom of a mini-map and trinket-laden pocket, and one of limited value, thus saving the heavy Euros for the much more valuable ritual of finding a pay toilet among the Roman ruins (and why is it that Italians never have to pee?). But SECNAV is no mere mortal, and change does not occupy his pockets, but rather one would find the odd golf tee, or perhaps a cigar cutter, monogrammed of course. No, SECNAV does what a titled monarchical figure does, and that is turn to his aide, who has magically appeared at his side to render any assistance, including coin dispensation.

A coin is indeed produced from the magical man-purse that every aide carries with no shame. But it is no simple coin. Nor is it even currency, at least not in the monetary sense. It is a Challenge Coin, in the grand tradition of every military unit of modern times – a custom-minted, beveled, bejeweled and ultimately bulky masterpiece of numismatics. This bronze coin is emblazoned with the flag of the office of the American Secretary of the Navy, complete with the raised signature of the current office holder, and the four-starred and anchored banner that is the flag of the post. This is no Euro.

To the gypsies and petty thieves present at Trevi, nothing goes unnoticed, least of all a vested God debarking from his land yacht, surrounded by uniformed serfs, and producing what appears to be a giant... gold... doubloon. This is a veritable gold ingot that everyone is instantly aware is about to be hurled into the fountain of Nicola Salvi's design. Even the ghost of Salvi is salivating at its readily apparent worth, amongst the cheap bronze cents that lie below the waves, untouched in their relative mediocrity.

What ensues as the coin is hurled purposefully into the public font is a full scale riot in the heart of Rome, not seen since the Coliseum roared, or perhaps since the wrongful conviction of the American tourist-harlot Amanda Knox. Gypsies, tourists, pick pockets, even casual passers-by are transfixed as the shining wafer glints towards its watery destination, and the mass of humanity begins to move toward it, with shouts of urgency to make way in 10 different languages. And just before water's entry, silence descends upon the square for a brief second, with even the pigeons gliding rather than flapping, awaiting the distinctive 'splish' as the coin angles into the hallowed waters.

And when it does, presently, the riot begins anew. The roar returns, and men, women and children of all variety hurl themselves into the fountain's depths, as if Neptune had cast them there with his own scepter; which essentially he has done through SECNAV's casual act of trite tradition. The waters are churned, as if they were the piranha infested waters of the muddy Amazon. The Carabineri are delighted, holstering their weapons, and lighting up their heaters, just as the violence begins to erupt. This, they signal, is Italian opera at its finest, and they are in the box seats.

And this is when the SECNAV's aide demonstrates why it was he who was chosen among many to fulfil the role of manservant to the most powerful naval figure on the globe. With no hesitation, and with full-throated yet controlled vigor, he turns to King Neptune and the wide-eyed American entourage, just now reaching for their cameras, and says: *"Mr. Secretary, it's time to Go."*

The effect is as miraculous as it is instantaneous. The SECNAV alights to his mobile throne as the Mrs. glances up from the pages of *Vogue Italia* (she is just now wondering why the Fiat was not airborne), the uniformed travelers take their positions in their sub-par chariots, the Carabineri grind their butts into the cobblestone and kick start their cycles – and the procession rockets from the square as quickly as it had come. In the mirrors of the Moto-guzzis, the riders glance back at the glory of Trevi, reminded that centuries have watched such Gods come and go, disrupting its peace but for a short time.

Some hours later, the Public Affairs Officer of the Secretary of the Navy sat at the hotel bar in his dress white uniform, sipping Prosecco and awaiting the evening's festivities. Across his back, unknown to him (but well known and pointed out to the rest of the staff by the Speechwriter) was a testament to the day's excitement – a perfect tire track from a Fiat motorcar, earned while the tunic was awaiting its rescue from the roundabout in the heart of Rome. It was to be a memorable visit to Rome after all. And forthwith, a lesson in how not to exhibit U.S. leadership abroad, post-9/11.

Leadership & the Career Inflection Point of Maximum Influence

A recent evening with a brother-in-law over glasses of good old American whiskey proved to be a charming and unexpected chance to compare and contrast our respective careers. Aside from being reminded once again that leadership fundamentals are essentially the same in the military and in business, he said something that resonated with my own perspective of leadership. He was at the point in his career when he felt he'd suddenly reached a level of experience and responsibility that was somewhat commanding, in a rather effortless way: after 18 years at a large bank he felt senior enough to have grasped the fundamentals of both the organization and the market; and yet still felt just junior enough to risk acting on that knowledge and present a contribution to the bank's mission outside of his own department.

I was reminded that the military assigns command responsibility to officers for significant units (ships, companies, squadrons) at about that same career point of 18 years. This is, I believe, an *inflection point of maximum influence*, that is universal across industries and professions, civilian and military. It's a point that most are not aware of (certainly *I* wasn't until Kentucky whiskey prompted me). Yet this point almost certainly represents great opportunity for an individual with higher career aspirations and a desire to impact the greater good; as well as an obligation for an organization to capture the passion and brilliance that employees at this inflection point represent.

What this alcohol-fueled analysis sets up is a simple bell curve, a somewhat lazy method to describe balance that is perhaps more phenomenological than it is quantitatively scientific. Nonetheless, the hypothesis is that over the course of a 30-plus year career, an individual is *most* productive for a few years around the 18-20 year mark, and much more so for a shining moment, than early on in her career, or afterwards as she slides down the back side of the curve.

This is not to say that people don't provide significant influence earlier or later in their careers; of course they do. But this essay is about the mean, and the inflection point that is just past about mid-career, that has some unique and powerful characteristics. A person has absorbed the uniqueness of the industry and the dynamics of the market he serves. He has been given some leadership responsibilities and knows the challenges of managing human behavior. He is still spending that wonderful care-free resource known as "other peoples' money." And he has not been around long enough to be too naïve, or too jaded, such that the corporate culture itself is a catalyst for indecision, and years of "the same mistakes" produces eye rolls rather than action. There remains a passion that is not yet overcome with too much experience and bureaucratic malaise.

Recognition of this brief but important plateau in a person's career is critical in my view, for maximum satisfaction and achievement of the individual *and* for impact to the organization. This is when, for instance, a former ship's captain of mine (18 years into his career), stood up to his commodore and took a risk, expending more than his allocated share of airborne training weapons during a critical exercise, ultimately leading to a fleet award for readiness despite an administrative reprimand for "excessive spending." And this is when my brother-in-law was allowed by his boss to devise a risky new program to capture significant market share – when those on the far side of the bell curve were highly resistant to embark on such a risk, despite the ample evidence presented.

Looking for these young "executives" and fostering their energy is highly incumbent upon the organization's most senior leadership – those on the right side of the curve. And it's equally important for career-ambitious individuals to recognize when they arrive at this inflection point, and maximize the potential it represents, for themselves and for the company.

Finally, there is another dynamic that can be brought to bear, when the perfect bell curve described here manifests itself, despite it being a challenging one for the individual. My banker-brother provided an added catalyst to his own 18-year inflection point, perhaps unbeknownst to him – that of servant leadership. He was willing to let his boss look good for much of his hard work and the ultimate proposal to the bank's senior leadership. This is a rare trait indeed, and one that exemplifies great humility and ultimately risk. As of this writing, we don't know if my relative's actions will spotlight an inflection point that proves my theory and lets him slide down the right side of the banking bell curve, allowing others to succeed behind him. But even if it doesn't he will have left a class example of servant leadership for others to emulate.

That's worth drinking to.

Leadership & 10 Military Principles That Translate to Business

After 21 years in the military, and nearly 20 years in business, it's apparent to me that effective leadership is largely the same in both worlds. The stakes may not be as high (though they often feel that way) but human behavior and market dynamics are the same. Everyone wants to win, and people doing the fighting want to believe in the mission. Here are 10 leadership fundamentals from the military that resonate in the business world.

1. _Be on time; all the time_. I was once part of a formation of four aircraft headed to a refueling destination, only to find the ship was not there, at the appointed time; trouble was, we were an hour early, not having adjusted our time zone. The miscalculation nearly led to four splashed helicopters. Your business relies on timing as well; of materials, labor and resources. Being precise is essential to running a tight ship – and a business. And being on time is also a signal of respect to your customers.

2. _Logisticians are critical; but they're not necessarily leaders_. In the military, logistics is paramount. It was Admiral King who said during WWII: _"I don't know what the hell this 'logistics' is that (General) Marshall is always talking about, but I want some of it."_ Similarly, in business, you're going nowhere without a well-oiled supply chain. But while you need to be realistic, don't let the "bean counters" run the show. Be realistic with the customer – but take some risks and be the visionary that can ultimately deliver value.

3. _Your sales force brings you to the fight; your production team wins it_. Ronald Reagan, as commander-in-chief, sold the "Star Wars" program to deter the Soviet Union and ultimately win the Cold War. Reagan knew the technology was not ready for prime time, but his vision was sufficiently bold to both check the enemy and inspire America. Similarly, a CEO needs to balance vision with a believable product. That means creating stretch goals while resourcing your team to achieve them.

4. *Bring added value, but first deliver what's asked for*. As an airborne asset during Desert Storm, we were able to bring advanced command and control to the battlefield; our helicopter's radar and sensor suite was second to none in the Arabian Gulf. But the allied commander wasn't buying what we were selling. He was looking for ordnance on target, and we couldn't deliver, unlike our British counterparts that had missiles on their aircraft. In business, the customer loves added value – but only when you bring the asked-for product to the table first.

5. *Trust your gut; but only if your gut knows the market*. The movie *"Heartbreak Ridge"* featured a Marine colonel who botched an attack in Grenada. The commanding general confronted him and discovered he'd been a supply officer most of his career. He then urged him to leave the infantry and go back to what he'd been good at. Business also needs informed leaders who understand the market they're in – who the competition is and where the mines are laid.

6. *Don't think you're the only one with a "secret weapon." You're not*. On today's battlefield adversaries have access to much of the same modern weaponry, sometimes facing an enemy they inadvertently equipped. In business, I hear entrepreneurs say: *"We're the only ones who make this."* That's almost never true and they often over-protect their IP to the point that marketing and sales are hindered. Patents are great, but speed to market is better. *"Innovate, sell, repeat"* is a worthy motto.

7. *A commander should serve his people; and let them conduct the mission*. Servant leadership is a hallmark of the U.S. Military. Effective commanding officers provide vision, inspiration and resources, and care for those who go in harm's way. Similarly, micromanagement is anathema to a business's culture. CEOs should delegate all day, while serving their employee and customer needs.

8. *Win the battles, not the war*. The captain of my destroyer once reminded me and my helicopter crew after a lengthy and involved brief during the first day of Desert Storm: *"The admiral wants a lot done. I just want you to deliver some*

SEALs to the beach and come back safely. We'll still be at war tomorrow." It's a good reminder that markets are pretty huge, and a small business only needs a fraction of a market's share to boost revenue.

9. *Ethics and quality matter*. Warfare is ugly, and in the heat of battle lines start to blur; it's just human nature. But becoming what one is fighting against defeats the purpose. In business, competition drives urgency; and urgency leads to exaggeration in marketing, cutting corners in quality, and worse. The real winners in war and business fight and produce for the common good along with achieving the mission and advancing the bottom line.

10. *Don't be distracted*. The peacetime military gets wrapped up with administration, non-combat training, paperwork and other things that don't really lead to readiness and mission success. In the Pentagon, we called it a *"self-licking ice cream cone."* It tastes good, but it's really only good for itself. Businesses can also become distracted with the latest HR initiative, strategic planning exercise and training program. But the customer awaits, and they're never distracted from what they want: quality and value.

Businesses can learn from the fundamentals of solid military leadership; and vice versa. Humans respond positively to these and other approaches whether they're working on a factory floor or flying off the deck of a destroyer. The customer is a mission, and mission success demands quality leadership.

Leadership & Moral Certitude

During the Iran Hostage Crisis of 1979-1981, one public figure stood out among all the rest in her steadfast belief that the hostages would ultimately be freed. She was neither a politician nor a bureaucrat; neither a journalist nor a pundit. She was both simply and substantially the wife of the senior diplomat held hostage at the U.S. Embassy in Tehran; and she was coincidentally my Mother. Penne Laingen was a public figure not by choice, but rather by unfortunate happenstance, and she exhibited Margaret Thatcher-level moral clarity and dignity throughout the 444 days of the crisis and beyond, in my admittedly biased view. That made her a leader of substance in the moment, and therefore a figure to whom many looked for information, guidance, and frankly for hope.

Since that era, we've entered a time of increased moral relativism in which leaders are often reluctant to take clear stances on contentious issues. They're told that many of those they lead come from a different world view and see things through different lenses. Often that's indeed true, and one's ability to listen, empathize, learn and adapt can *absolutely* enhance a leader's credibility and influence. But there are times when a leader needs to remain true to core beliefs... ideals that she knows to be sacrosanct, despite relativist thought from seemingly credible sources.

For Penne Laingen, equivocation from the White House, the State Department, media figures and others over "past sins" of American foreign policy, or "legitimate grievances" of the Iranian people were certainly recognized as part of the conversation. But she knew and voiced with certitude – more than any leading public figure at the time – that while those perspectives had worth, they paled in comparison to the moral and legal breaches that were manifest in the wholesale abandonment of diplomatic immunity and human rights that the taking of hostages demonstrated.

In those efforts, in those troubled times, Penne Laingen was lonely. She was quite literally almost entirely alone as a public figure voicing her convictions with such certitude. Her creation of the original "yellow ribbon," now a ubiquitous symbol for so many other causes, with so many other colors, embodied the purity of her message – one of hope above all, but also one that reflected her conviction that right and wrong was still a relatively simple binary choice for some things in life, and that they would always be so.

Effective leadership is often a lonely endeavor. Sometimes we know that our decisions will be questioned in equal measure to our character, and the temptation to back down from what we know is right can be overwhelming. But with leadership comes an obligation to be centered and true to fundamental tenets of right and wrong. No amount of modernism or progressivism, however well-intentioned, can change them. Effective leaders are courageous in their convictions and are unabashed as they wear the ribbons which guide their morality.

Leadership & It's Not About You

Today marks the 99th birthday of my late Dad, an exemplar in my life for the principle of leadership being about those you serve – not about you. And on this day I was witness to another example of that selfless value: Olympian *Tamyra Mensah-Stock*. More about this champion in a moment...

When I was a young junior officer in the Navy, I was assigned as the officer-in-charge for the powerplants division of a helicopter squadron, ostensibly responsible for the performance and welfare of some 35 enlisted Sailors on sea duty, most of whom had been in the Navy far longer than I had. After several weeks of going through the motions as their "leader," freshly out of college and flight school, the division Chief took me aside in the hangar bay of the aircraft carrier. *"Lieutenant,"* he said, *"You're doing just fine... we hear you... you're saying all the right things. But maybe think about listening more to all the right things your Sailors have to say, too. They're pretty good at what they do."*

That was a wake up call for me, a reminder that the division was the division, not me. I was really there to serve them, not the other way around. And the Chief was a walking, talking example of servant leadership that I could see in a whole new light. His comment didn't include himself in any way – except of course as a mentor for me, and as an advocate for his Sailors.

Back to our 2021 American Olympian, Tamyra Mensah-Stock, who won gold for herself and the United States in women's wrestling. When asked *"How does it feel to represent your country like this?"*, this daughter of a first-generation immigrant, hugging the Stars and Stripes wrapped around her, responded by saying this: *"I love representing the U.S. I freaking love living there."*

Mensah-Stock didn't talk about her own amazing accomplishment that was the result of years of arduous discipline and training. Instead she remarked on the gratitude she has for the opportunity she was given, and for her love of the country that provided it. And she went on to say that the prize money she would receive as a gold medalist would go to funding her Mom's dream of owning a food truck, not her own dreams. Her championship was not about her. It was about those who made her accomplishment possible, and about her gratitude for it.

For me, I continue to need these constant reminders of pure, unfettered, selfless leadership, from my own Dad, to my first division Chief in the Navy, to American Olympian Mensah-Stock. Selflessness is not a human trait that comes naturally for most of us. Thankfully we have those for whom it does, if we only let ourselves learn from their example.

Leadership & Optimism ~ and Its Relationship to Joy

The very best leaders exude optimism; though they may not be inherently optimistic. Let me explain my assertion by psycho-analyzing myself. First, I'm certainly not a pessimist. Let's dispense with *any* connection between pessimism and good leadership right away, as it's the certain belief that the *worst* will occur. Rather, I'm a realist... not an optimist. I wish I was the latter, but I'm not. I ascribe that reality to being a helicopter pilot, wherein I have a built-in belief that the flux capacitor is getting ready to fail and the machine is about to come apart. It happens rarely, but when it does, it's usually spectacular in a way that fixed wing aviators don't fully grasp.

Over time, the machines that I flew generally didn't come apart. Or rather they did, quite often, but never spectacularly. So I came to believe that there was at least some cause for optimism in completing the mission. Experience and at least some luck changed my outlook. Realists like me are often originally pessimists who cheated fate long enough such that they can graduate to a better state.

But for truly effective leaders, the best among us, that's not enough. Those whom we ask to follow our lead need to believe their efforts will achieve the most favorable outcome, every time; which is what the textbook definition of optimism is. They won't truly believe that unless they perceive a vibrant optimism within those who lead them. But what about those imposters like myself, who aren't truly optimists? How can we at least be perceived as such?

This leads to my next level of psycho-analysis. One can be realistic about risks, but still exude optimism... but only if one has joy in the work. And I mean full, unapologetic love and gratitude for one's chosen profession and the mission at hand. That you can't fake. The very best leaders I've had may have been realists, but I perceived them as optimists through and through, probably because of the authentic joy they had for their work and the gratitude for those they led in that service.

One of the Marines who died in the Afghanistan withdrawal was *Sergeant Nicole Gee*. I didn't know her at all, but like many onlookers to the debacle, we were fortunate to witness various scenes of her life immediately before her passing. In every instance, we saw pure joy in her demeanor. It was so strong that it came across in spades even through still photographs and sparing quotes. There's no doubt in my mind that *Sergeant Gee* was a joyful person who reveled in her work; and that her spirit led her to exude optimism. Perhaps she was actually more of a realist – who knows? But her rare meritorious promotion to sergeant just weeks before her death was testament to a true leader who exuded an optimism that was clearly multiplied by an authentic, joyful embrace of her service.

We can be realistic as leaders, even to the point of being cautious in some things. But unless we deliver an optimistic roadmap for the best outcomes, those we lead won't perform to their potential. And achieving that means living and exuding an authentic joy for the mission at hand.

Leadership & The False Luxuries of "Peacetime" Leadership

One of the greatest maritime novels of all time is Nicholas Monsarrat's *"The Cruel Sea."* Written in 1951, it describes the perils faced by the tiny escort vessels of the Royal Navy charged with protecting merchant convoys in the North Atlantic during the early years of World War II. More aptly described it is a treatise on effective wartime leadership during times of extreme stress and change, following years of peace.

The protagonist's new captain, young and inexperienced, is thrust into command of the tiny corvette, with an equally novice crew. The story ultimately makes clear his exemplary leadership, foreshadowed by this note of self-awareness as he steps aboard for the first time:

"At the moment he had, as his novel responsibility, a new job, a new ship and a new crew. In theory he was proud of them all..."

In the business world, much of our time is spent in relative peace as well, before the inevitable high seas of a merger, major policy changes or significant personnel turnover. During these times of calm and prosperity, we sometimes stray from the enduring, core principles of effective leadership. Long-delayed programs can be installed, and we are better able to indulge in experiments that we hope will boost both morale and productivity. Sometimes those things are worthy, as we have all benefited from the tenets of diversity and inclusion (D&I), at least once they were unburdened from affirmative action programs. The U.S. Military itself essentially created and perfected D&I beginning with President Truman's Integration of the Armed Forces in 1948 (Executive Order 9981).

Like all things driven by human-centric good intentions however, our peacetime indulgences can go too far. The new addition of "equity" to D&I is a prime example. One definition of equity as applied to the corporate world is *"…recognizing that we do not all start from the same place and must acknowledge and make adjustments to imbalances."* (National Association of Colleges and Employers). "Making adjustments" sounds relatively benign and many important ones can and should be made, as we do with disabilities. But business has a bottom line that must be driven by core leadership principles – principles that reward merit, by advancing employees who perform to the mission and its high standards over all else. Can they co-exist? Certainly; but as harsh as it sounds, the balance between merit and equity has to strongly fall to the former. For those of us leading in both the military and in business, the negative consequences that come from mis-managing this balance are rapid and apparent.

Our fictional Royal Navy captain could have continued to indulge in peacetime luxuries as well. But he understood that only in theory was he was proud of his entire crew... even perhaps initially making adjustments for those whose circumstances put them at a disadvantage. But combat is always right over the next wave, and advancing one's crew based principally on merit will always win the war and grow the business.

Leadership & Perspective

Perspective is an interesting and complicated subject, as it applies to so many things, and is ultimately measured by the person doing the perceiving. So it's a highly personal concept in the end. But as perspective relates to leadership, how *you* perceive things is being perceived by those you lead, whether you like it or not. I don't mean to be arcane, so to simplify what I'm saying, let me convey this: as a leader, you are constantly being measured by your reaction to things. In that context, it's important to focus on your perspective – ultimately how you react to things… especially, let's say, crises. You are being watched, and judged by your reaction to them.

One of my last days on active duty, as commander of a training squadron, brought this into sharp focus for me. I had the privilege to work for a wing commodore (essentially the "owner" of all the squadrons on base), who had a solid grasp of perspective in life, in my opinion. Knowing that, and wanting to provide him an unorthodox "thank you" for his leadership as I retired, I sent him a fairly unorthodox invitation: would he like to join me at one of our remote, outlying fields at the base of the rudimentary control tower (it was a grass helicopter strip) and observe flight operations, while eating a fried chicken lunch in rocking chairs?

He replied in the affirmative, and we proceeded to the field in our rented Navy training chopper, shutting down at about noon – where my most junior officer had pre-staged the rocking chairs, box lunches, and the wing commander's flag. My order of mint julips went unheeded, sadly (we were in the deep South, after all). Despite the oversight, we had a delightful "summit" with iced teas as a backup, while observing the Commodore's aircraft from the two squadrons performing their multiple touch and go's, and other maneuvers to the grass field on a lovely late spring day.

Word, of course, had leaked out, that the Commodore was watching flight operations, and the instructor pilots and students were on their best behavior, so to speak. Toward the end of our lunch, however, one of the aircraft spectacularly performed a hard landing just yards from the Commodore in his rocking chair, spreading the skids slightly – after which the crew shut down the aircraft and walked sheepishly toward the control tower. The Commodore, never wavering from his comfortable rocking chair, held up his glass of iced tea to the crew and saluted them, saying: *"Lived to fight another day, gentlemen."*

Perhaps it was the rocking chairs, or the fried chicken that had relaxed him; but I choose to believe that we had a leader in the Commodore who had a solid, healthy sense of perspective in life. He understood what was in his control, and what was not, and he thereby reflected a sense of calm to those who were striving for perfection, but occasionally fell short.

Should you care what people think about your sense of perspective as a leader? I think so; and I equate it to balance – that an effective leader should have a firm grasp of what truly matters for the organization and what it takes to achieve excellence – but that occasionally humans fail, while they are striving for it.

Leadership & Perspective II

A Navy helicopter crept its way up the Potomac River near the Pentagon at just under 100 feet, enshrouded in a sudden, heavy, early-morning fog. Just a mere mile or so from the iconic building's landing pad, the crew eventually came to a tentative hover over the roiling, muddy water, the multi-million dollar aircraft's sophisticated sensors useless without visual cues in getting it to its final destination – so very close, but for now unattainable.

Getting low on fuel, the aircraft commander nudged the craft toward the riverbank where a jogging trail was barely visible through the haze. Once there, the aircrewman slid open the main cabin door and yelled down to a jogger over the din of the turbine engines and whirring blades, some 40 feet below. *"Where are we?!"* he boomed.

The reply from the nonplussed runner was both as clear as it was unhelpful: *"You're in a helicopter!"*

This is a *nearly*-accurate sea story to illustrate an important point for effective leaders: when communicating critical information, the sender's frame of reference may not quite match that of the receiver, and may lead to serious misunderstanding. It's a ubiquitous problem even for the best of leaders who believe they communicate clearly and often. Aristotle urged a robust, meaningful connection by building credibility, appealing to emotion and logic and even considering the timing of one's delivery (ethos, pathos, logos, and kairos). But the most sage of the ancient philosophers found out that even all of that isn't sufficient. Aristotle's own teacher Plato was sentenced to death, after all, for "corrupting" young people with his ideas. His frame of reference didn't exactly align with the ruling class.

The answer isn't a perfect one, but it boils down to immersing oneself, somehow, in the lived experience of those being led. How are they living, what are they feeling, and what are the direct impacts to them of decisions their leaders have made in the past, and are making today? Aristotle's appeal to "pathos" comes close (emotion); but knowing the *root causes* of that emotion is a next-level leadership exercise that can pay even greater dividends. An example that comes to mind from my Navy experience was that of the disgruntlement families felt regarding the length and frequency of deployments of their service members. Years of experience revealed that negative feelings about their shared sacrifice stemmed not just from the time away – that was expected – but more from the lack of *predictability* regarding the Sailor's schedule. The families just wanted to know when they would be on their own, so they could plan accordingly. Understanding that (the real impact of difficult leadership decisions on the families of those being led) provided a congruent frame of reference, and made for more decipherable and respectful communications.

Now back to our wayward helicopter… to make a long story short, the aircrew assumed that the jogger was a Pentagon employee and that they were therefore close to their destination; because he exhibited well-known traits of such employees: while his answer to where they were was technically correct, it was also essentially useless in the moment, and admittedly sarcastic.

Thankfully more specific queries ultimately led them to the landing pad just as the helicopter's low fuel lights flashed their warnings. It was a shared experience none of the crew wanted to repeat; but nonetheless a solid reminder of the importance of understanding not only one's own perspective, but that of those being led.

Phenomenological Leadership

I was introduced to the word "phenomenological" thanks to a friend's PhD dissertation; the word was in fact in the title. There are varied definitions, but essentially a phenomenological approach is one of *"intentional study of lived experiences."* I found that interesting, admittedly not for its definition but because it's seven syllables and I desperately wanted to use it in some way. But it wasn't until this past week that I fully grasped its importance in the context of leading diverse organizations... which most now are.

The realization came when a former student called for advice. He is about to take on a role in a new company, leading others for the first time; 15 people he's never met. That's pretty daunting the first time it happens, and it took me back to my first leadership assignment in the Navy, as division officer for a maintenance branch with a similar number of enlisted Sailors. The Chief took me aside and said something to the effect of: *"They're all pretty different, Sir. You'd best figure them out, than the other way around."* I didn't know it at the time, but I'm pretty sure the Chief was telling me to conduct a phenomenological study of the men and women in my division – to get to know their individual lived experiences, both in the service, and before. By doing that, I could provide leadership that was better informed by the nuances of those being led, from their motivations, to their unique skills, to their perceptions of risk, to their abilities to contribute to the team.

That's not ground-breaking. It's just a need to establish a connection with those you lead that goes beyond transactional leadership, to more transformational leadership, where things happen because people are inspired to act, not ordered to act.

Academia further informs us that phenomenological research can prove to be *"highly qualitative, which makes it hard to present the findings in a fashion practitioners would consider to be useful."* But we're not presenting findings to practitioners - we *are* the practitioners. And for effective leadership practitioners in the real world, qualitative judgments trump quantitative ones all day long. And that's phenomenal. Or phenomenological, as it were.

Leadership & Power From Below

An old squadron mate and I recently connected after 25 years, and the conversation centered on our time together flying off a Navy destroyer in the Adriatic Sea. Before the conversation naturally devolved to tales of liberty in various Mediterranean ports, we discussed our own experiences relating to leadership. Together we've had a combined half-century of service in various commands, in the Navy and Air Force (he transferred to that service mid-career); yet we easily agreed that one six-month period on said destroyer gave us our best example of command leadership, in the form of the ship's captain.

Why, we asked, was that so? The captain's positive, engaging personality explained a lot of it. Life on a small ship is often described as *"being in prison with a chance of drowning;"* so a happy warden certainly helps, especially one who constantly reminded us, cheerfully, that our sentence was making a difference in the world. But something else stood out. The captain's place is generally on the bridge nearly 24/7, essentially the highest point on the ship, a place from which to exercise authority and "fight the ship." And certainly our captain was there when he needed to be. But more often than not he was below decks: in the engine room, in the combat information center, eating in the crew's galley, in the helicopter hangar, and even in the bosun's locker, a place where officer's rarely dare to tread, much less the commanding officer.

While in those dark recesses of the warship, our captain was not generally commanding or leading or exercising his authority in any overt way. He was the furthest thing from a micro-manager, in fact. Rather, he was there to learn, to relate, to empathize, to teach, to cajole, to understand, and even to serve. While there his positivity was infectious, and in fact one could hear his booming laughter several decks removed, as he learned about his shipmates, and genuinely shared in their misery and in their joy in equal measure.

We discussed all of this, my former co-pilot and I, and then he neatly summed it up for me with a phrase that expressed a level of wisdom I admittedly thought was incapable of coming from an Air Force officer: our captain understood that command leadership was about *"authority from above, and power from below."*

I'd never heard that phrase, and still don't know if he had just coined it. Nevertheless, it neatly summed up for me what effective, servant leadership really is. Our captain routinely stood on the bridge and exercised authoritative command. On a U.S. Navy ship, that's perfunctory, of course; but in our captain's case that authority came with tremendous respect from the crew, as they understood he had a mutual respect for the *true* source of power of his warship – not his own statutory authority, but ultimately the work and sacrifice of the Sailors serving well below where he stood. When that happens, perfunctory authority is transformed, and becomes powerful authority. Our destroyer was the "go-to" ship in the battle group. All these years later, I now know why.

Leadership & Quiescence

Most leaders are put in leadership positions because they can handle the complexity, chaos and confusion that comes with positions of authority; and when they get there, they tend to be assigned added responsibility, and even volunteer for more. Yet a common complaint among them is lack of time – to answer emails, to manage projects, to plan ahead… even to just sit and think. The result is a sense of foundering and losing control.

I recall an analogous situation while hovering over the back of a destroyer in the Mediterranean some years ago. We had launched from a stable deck four hours before, returning to a ship tossed like a cork in a sea state of seven. Seven, on the Douglas Sea Scale of 0-9 means 20-30 foot waves. It's dangerous for a ship of any size; much more so for a helicopter trying to alight on a small one. We thankfully learned that ships on high seas experience a *"quiescent"* period – the definition of which is a *"state or period of inactivity or dormancy."* The ship's pitch and roll largely cease, generally at the bottom of a swell, for a blessed few seconds. We used it to drop the aircraft on deck, before the stern could fall away or pitch up into us. Our aim was accurate as we slammed into the "bear trap," with just enough time to receive high point chains from brave, untethered Sailors on deck, to further prevent us from rolling off into the sea.

Leaders, like aircrew in high seas, should seek the quiescent periods, too. We need time to settle our minds, to calm our spirits, to plan the next move. They allow for us to land safely back where we need to, anchored to where we were headed in the first place. These periods exist, in the busiest of roles if we look for them; though sometimes it seems like they never come. Ideally, then, an effective leader plans them for himself, to become grounded once again in what really matters.

Quiescence is equally important for those we lead. The Navy actually schedules the occasional *"Ropeyarn Sunday"* for its Sailors out at sea, where 24/7 operations for six months is common. The tradition began with the need to dedicate time to mending and splicing the many ropes on tall ships, and became personal time for the crew to do chores and even have some leisure activities. The officers understood the need for everyone in the chain of command to experience quiet, and calm. Not too much, though – otherwise Sailors and aircrew start to ask themselves what the hell they're doing floating around in the middle of nowhere and getting sick in horrific sea states. We can't have that!

Lead into the highest of seas... but make the most of the quiescent periods when they appear.

Leadership & Restoring the Joy

These are uniquely challenging times for leaders. There's a growing sense of disquiet in our culture, and it's easy to succumb to a general feeling of malaise. Our popular culture can lecture us all it wants about alleged systemic inequities and outdated cultural constructs of what constitutes excellence and generates joy for those we lead. The problem is almost none of it is actually true; and where it is true, the basics of sound leadership to achieve excellence aren't actually any different than they've ever been.

We can be tempted to sit back and wait for others to improve things. After all, isn't it the result of someone else's actions, not our own? Perhaps, to some degree. But while history can be re-invented by a distorted popular culture; human nature cannot. So the responsibility for leadership is ours alone, using the tools that we know to be timeless. Restoring the joy to an organization and to individuals is a three-step process of leadership, in my view.

First, we need to bring things down to where *we* are, and what *we* know to be right. In another essay I spoke about a Marine sergeant many years ago who overheard several of us young midshipmen complaining about all manner of things after a long training patrol in the high desert, all of which involved our grievances with the President, the Secretary of the Navy and various high ranking commanders. *"Remember, gentlemen,"* he said as he strolled by our campfire, *"All leadership is local."* Our responsibility is ultimately just the here and now, to improve things where *we* are, to ensure those we lead have what they need to excel, to produce – and yes, to be joyful.

Second, there is a place for empathy, and a need to find effective ways to reduce the stress that is naturally present in challenging circumstances. The commander of the Navy's amphibious ship USS John P. Murtha recently found a creative way to do just that by making a giant pinata out of shipboard materials and filling it with thousands of donated treats and items from the ship's store. It was hung in the cavernous hangar bay and savagely attached by the Sailors... a simple, but wildly popular break from the norms of daily life aboard ship that signaled an understanding of the stress and uncertainty the crew was experiencing.

Finally, we need to be inspirational; to be the face of the excellence and joy we want for our organization. In a recent graduate-level class on Risk Communications my co-instructor and I were blessed with a remarkable panel of experts who shared their best practices from industry, academia and government. The speaker from industry has the awesome, and somewhat daunting, title *"Director, Reputation Management"* (for a Fortune 100 corporation). She described her exhausting daily routine of pre- and post-crisis work, from cyber-attacks to social media monitoring to physical security challenges at hundreds of global locations. One student asked her how she stayed so upbeat and positive despite being responsible for managing overwhelmingly negative tasks. Her response was instantaneous: *"That's easy... my job is to restore the joy."*

I found that to be inspiring – an especially positive take on one's role in the organization, as well as being a reminder for leaders to keep people more focused on the mission and its positive outcomes, and less on the often-thankless work that achieves it. Lead at your level, and manage what you can manage, knowing what you know to be true. Truly understand and empathize with those you serve. And perhaps most importantly lead with the joy you hope to inspire in others.

Leadership & Risks – Real Leaders Take Them (II)

In the first volume I penned an article about leadership and the need to take risks. Since then, a pandemic re-focused how we each perceive risk to our own safety and evaluate others on how they do the same. Through that lens we've all admittedly become somewhat judgmental regarding risk, but it's nonetheless caused me to reflect on what we're willing to risk on behalf of *others* – a hallmark of servant leadership.

When I was in flight school, I was the beneficiary of a servant leader who had enough faith in my abilities to risk his own personal safety on my safe-for-solo flight. I had flown my first 11 flights with a Navy instructor for whom I was his first student; a wonderful officer, but one who was perhaps more encouraging than demanding, when in fact I very much needed the latter. Airsick on every flight, I could not even land the aircraft un-assisted after 11 flights. Flight 12, the safe-for-solo check ride, was the first flight with a different instructor, this time a Marine officer. He read my performance record carefully and said: *"Ensign, I will be sitting on my hands this entire flight, and closing my eyes in the landing pattern. If you get airsick, or fail to land this plane, you're out of the program and will be driving a ship in a matter of weeks."*

Knowing what I know of Marines, I have little doubt that the captain was true to his word. I didn't hear from him during the entire flight, and he may in fact have been napping at one point. I didn't get airsick, and I landed the plane multiple times like I'd been doing it my entire life. They still sent me to helicopters eventually, but that's another story; and I did end up driving ships also (yet another story).

What's the point of this anecdote? Effective leaders take risks, not just personal ones to advance their own careers, but to advance the welfare and careers of others. My instructor could easily have guarded the controls and summarily sent me down a different career path. But he took a risk to his own safety, and perhaps to his reputation, and advanced me towards my wings of gold. It wasn't until eighteen years later, as a flight instructor myself, that I realized the risks that Marine had taken, and the servant leadership that he demonstrated.

Real, effective leaders take risks – not just for themselves, but also on behalf of others.

Leadership & Working Your "Scan"

One of the hardest things we had to learn in flight school was flying in Instrument Meteorological Conditions (IMC): the art of flying blind, in the clouds, and at night. Particularly in an inherently unstable helicopter, there's a LOT to concentrate on, just to keep the craft upright and flying where you intend to go, safely. One has to keep up a continuous "scan" – moving the eyes rapidly between "airspeed, attitude and ball" (the airspeed indicator, the gyro and the balanced flight indicator), while making constant corrections based on what that scan is telling you. And that's just to avoid disaster. One also has to incorporate other variables into that primary scan, like navigating, monitoring the engines and rotors, communicating to the crew and air traffic control, and of course handling the random emergency procedure introduced by the instructor.

You learn very quickly in that environment that everything matters, all the time; because as soon as you move your scan to attend to one variable, all of the others are going where you don't want them to go. All of them, all the time.

That's the way it is with leadership, too. We focus on one project, or work on assisting one employee, or listen to the voice of one customer and each of those likely improves for a time. Meanwhile, by definition, you're neglecting everything else. And everything else is important and is changing. Good leaders, then, develop a constantly moving scan, like a wary helicopter pilot on a dark and stormy night. They are constantly shifting their attention from one important task to the next; from one valued employee to the other.

But what if you're really important and you're flying a really complex aircraft? Isn't that why they invented autopilot? Flight school generally didn't let us use autopilot, because we were being prepared for the worst situation possible, when the autopilot has failed. Once in the Fleet, we could select the autopilot and do what every respectable helicopter pilot then does - drink coffee and tell lies about our past exploits, which of course were legion. And what if you're running a really big and important business? We have autopilot there, too: department heads to which you can delegate; HR departments that can handle needy employees; and sales teams that can gather voice of the customer.

But just like the autopilot on an aircraft, those failsafes require a scan too, and they sometimes fail to live up to a leader's needs; not often, and usually not completely, but they sometimes fail nonetheless. And when they do, the pilot – the leader himself – is ultimately the last resort. That failsafe consists of a healthy, constantly moving scan among all the important things in a business, which is to say *everything*. And it also includes a healthy culture that has been created over lots of flights in instrument conditions, and walk-arounds in your business... a culture that includes things like delegation of duties and responsibilities, building up of trust, and allowing for diversity of thought and the fostering of initiative.

I once had a grizzled old Navy contract flight instructor debrief me after a particularly dismal performance in a helicopter simulator, in which I flew the thing into the ocean, quite spectacularly. He said to me, through his wad of chewing tobacco in a southern drawl: "You'll get it... eventually, Ensign. You're almost average, after all. But here's the secret: If you always fly your machine like it doesn't *want* to fly; then it will fly like it *wants* to fly."

Thanks to him I can't really ever relax in a cockpit. But it was pretty sound advice, nonetheless, and I like to think I have a pretty healthy scan going in business and in life.

Leadership & The Scent of a Warship

Not my usual article on leadership... but as we all finally wake up to the realization that masks don't work, here's an article about the power of scent - dedicated to those who sail in defense of liberty.

I reported aboard an old U.S. Navy Adams class destroyer in Pearl Harbor as a first class midshipman in the summer of 1982. It was an experience that I can viscerally re-live in my head to this day; and most notably because of the unique scents I experienced, that provide the most vivid memories of that period in my life.

It began by arriving in Hawaii for the first time, and back then it meant actually walking down a boarding ladder, outdoors, at Honolulu International. Hawaii is another planet, most notably for the hibiscus and salt air in the fresh, tropical breeze. One instantly is conscious of breathing as nowhere else on the Earth, and the reminder of the deliciousness of life that it brings, which isn't a thing anywhere else. It just isn't. Perhaps getting lei'd by a stewardess – not a flight attendant in 1982, but an attractive female stewardess, thank you – as you depart the plane had something to do with it.

But as wonderful as that was, it's eclipsed by the scent of a modern warship. It begins as one walks down the piers, which are actually concrete finger piers that still to this day have wooden pilings layered with creosote – a delicious anti-fungal coating that evokes the essence of tar, only sweeter and more layered in its consistency. Together with the heavy, rotting ropes that surround them and the pier's many rusting iron bollards, the odor mixes with seagull feces and is mere foreplay before walking up and over the brow of a destroyer, and on to the holy premises of the quarterdeck itself. This is the ship's lobby – the lobby of a boutique hotel into which only a few, select travelers are invited.

There, one experiences a nearly orgasmic explosion of odors, all of which are glorious in their complexity and richness. To be clear, the first-timer has no idea what he's taking in – yet. For now, he's focusing on trying to emote calm professionalism, preparing to salute the ensign far astern before turning to salute and address the officer-of-the-deck, requesting permission to come aboard an active ship-of-the-line. But it's in the subconscious, and it's there to stay... that inexplicable blend of olfactory goodness that only a warship can produce.

First, there's the smell of steel. If you don't think steel has a smell, then you've never been aboard a warship. It's very real, and generally masculine. On older warships it begins to take on a delightful tang of decay... oxidation accelerated by salt water's humid attack that occurs relentlessly on the steel plates of the vessel. I give odds that a seasoned boatswain's mate could tell you the difference between various types of metal and their scents; or at the very least could verify that steel is an aphrodisiac. They're not bright, boatswain's mates... but they live life to the fullest, that I can assure you.

Second, there's the smell of electronics. Again, this is a modern warship, and it's essentially a floating computer... or a steel container jammed with computers, better stated. Electronics smell also. It's an odor that puts one on edge, in a sense... because you get the feeling that there's something shorting out, something burning, something about to catastrophically arc and spark and explode. It won't – usually – but it reminds you that it's dangerous as hell, like pain in the body – nature's way of saying that something just isn't right. And it's usually not; but it's a delightful odor nonetheless.

Third, the ship's galley hits you, as you transcend even one deck lower. The food on a destroyer is deplorable, generally (you have to be on a cruiser or some other more worthy ship-of-the-line to get cuisine rather than food), but there are exceptions. Most notably there is the fresh-baked bread. A Paris bistro couldn't hold a baguette to the smell of a fresh-baked loaf of pure, simple white bread on a destroyer. It rises to the top of the steel and electronics and overlays it with a hot crust of delight that one can breathe in throughout the ship.

Fourth, chemicals and fuels, and all things liquid and gassy and un-naturally man-made permeate every inch of a warship's length and beam. This is a multi-faceted OSHA violation that no level of inspection and report of remedies could rectify; there are just too many of them: paints and solvents, de-greasers and chem-wipes, aviation and diesel fuels, rocket fuel and solid missile propellant, deck remover and relative bearing grease. It's a slurry that if combined would make nuclear material critical mass seem like child's play. All in all, it's a tar pit from hell, and it's unforgettably ripe and real.

Finally, there's an undercurrent that is more subtle, far less pungent, and much more natural – but perhaps because of its innocence, overcomes all, and layers the aforementioned such that the totality is ultimately sublime. It's the smell of the sea itself – the salt, the sun, the fish, the gulls, the froth, the foam… the waves themselves. Even here, nestled far into the recesses of Pearl Harbor, the Pacific's totality blends the cacophony of all these odors of a modern warship. It's ultimately a soothing, cathartic effect of combination, that allows a Sailor to fully enjoy the uniqueness of a warship and its man-made affectations, while appreciating that the vessel belongs to nature's vastness; as that is where she will ultimately head, belonging amidst the heave of the swell on the high seas.

Leadership & Time

Leadership comes with lots of responsibility and accountability; and much of that relates to time management in some way. Here are ten temporal tricks to make sure your leadership is doing justice to that precious commodity we call time:

1) We've all heard the saying: the days drag by, but the years fly by. Indeed they do. Trust me, at my age you wake up every day with that in mind. Great leaders use this to remember to truly "be in the moment." Focus less on next week and next year. They're on their way no matter what you do. Instead, focus on the here and now. What do the people you serve need *right now* to be successful? What are they saying about their present needs? Are you acting on their behalf now, or are you *only* planning for a better future?

2) Time and money are everything; and in fact they're quite related. They are commodities that you can't manufacture. But you can manage them. Step away from the maelstrom for a moment and examine where you're spending your time, and why, and whom with? It's a virtual certainty that the balance is askew in some way. Reset your time blocks to align with your objectives and your values.

3) Effective leaders are on time – period. Not early, and certainly not late. *On Time*. Not being on time signals all kinds of things to those you serve and lead, including poor judgement, sloppy management, and most egregiously a lack of respect for *their* time. Don't ever forget that you are not as important as they are, and that their time matters even more than yours… by a long shot.

4) Give the gift of time. As leaders we look for ways to reward our employees, and it's generally in the form of money, praise and promotions. Those are all good, but remember that a

valuable gift is time itself. Award an hour off, or a day off here and there, just because, or for some specific achievement. Want to make it even more powerful? Give them overtime for that time if they pledge they'll give it to their family or their community; accountants be damned.

5) There's a time and a place. Another temporal dynamic is *timing*. Aristotle is known for his three modes of persuasion: Ethos, Pathos and Logos. Less well known is that he included a fourth rhetorical imperative – *"Kairos,"* the Greek word for the opportune moment. It was a reminder that even the most important or righteous of messages may not be best presented if the time isn't right. Leaders need to look for those opportune moments at which their messages will be best received.

6) Think about time in an *analog* way. I've always been a fan of analog watches over digital ones. This is not a backward mode of thought, at least in my view; but rather it affords the mind a contextual dynamic… to see the span of a minute or an hour within a temporal frame. That allows for the ability to better ration time as the valuable commodity that it is.

7) There's no time like the present. Really good leaders take on too much; or better stated, they are recognized as good leaders and they're assigned too much. Either way, we're often overwhelmed with too many tasks and too little time. Procrastination is never the answer, however, as the in-box starts to overflow. It's a balance, to be sure, but I've found that getting most things done *now* is generally better than putting things off.

8) Other peoples' time is valuable. This is a corollary to #3 – you're not that important, and those you lead value time as much as you do. Think about what you're asking of people with regard to meetings and emails and expectations and deadlines. The axiom *"be brief; be bright; be gone"* was created by those who have suffered through laborious

leadership lectures and such. Get your expectations out there, and then get off the stage.

9) The space-time continuum changes when you're the one speaking. As a former speechwriter, I know this as surely as I know that time advances only in one direction. If you think you're going to take 10 minutes, you'll take 20. So plan for five if you want to take 10. And relatedly, remember that 20 minutes is a magic number. After 20 minutes, people stop listening even to gifted speakers. Bottom line with any time period: *speak less and listen more*.

10) Finally, give *yourself* some time. The work-life balance is largely a myth for really effective leaders... but only because it's about as real as the proverbial unicorn. Embrace that reality, and then exercise some selfishness now and then. Unplug, immerse yourself in things that take you to a different space-time continuum, and free your mind from time. It won't really work, but it's a healthy pursuit, nonetheless.

Time is valuable. It's time to quit reading this, and focus on serving those you lead. Time will judge your sincere efforts on their behalf.

Leadership & Truisms

I'm a sucker for lists: making them, checking things off when completed, adding new items – even writing things down after they're already done, just so I can delight in making that check mark. It's pathological, but there's no cure. A business colleague recently asked what I believe to be "truisms" when it comes to leadership, in life and in business. My quick answer with two or three items then developed into a days-long list; one that I'm still adding to. Here are my **Leadership Truisms**, as of this writing (and if you don't like lists, scroll on to something else. After all there's no real context or depth here. It's just a list).

- Get over yourself. Everyone is already over you.

- You will only succeed as a leader if you want everyone around you to succeed.

- A leader can never have a bad day; or rather you can, but you can never show it.

- People want affirmation as much as they want pay and benefits; in some ways even more.

- Your time is far less valuable than the time of those you lead.

- You are not the only firm that does what you do.

- Being late is never OK. Not for those you lead. Not for customers. Not for yourself.

- Give people leeway, but never on questions of ethics and safety.

- Mistakes and failures can, and should be forgiven, but only if they're understood, corrected and lead to positive change.

- Don't ever be late; and don't allow it from people you lead. Timeliness is next to Godliness.

- Effective leaders listen a lot more than they act.

- Good leaders delegate everything except accountability.

- If you care about the credit more than the results, you don't deserve the credit.

- You are accountable for everything, even though you're not responsible for everything.

- Measure everything. But know that some things can't actually be measured.

- Metrics matter. Character matters more.

- Activity is not an outcome. Activity matters, but not as much as outcomes.

- Never fully trust anyone who works less hard than you do; and know that you're not fully trusted if you don't work harder than those for whom you work.

- Be willing to invest more than those who invest in you, in time, effort and money.

- Spend much more time on general principles than on specific tasks. If the strategy is sound, the tactics almost write themselves.

- Everything is important; but not everything deserves all of your attention.

- Everyone is important, and everyone deserves all of your attention, all the time.

- Your example is everything. And everyone is always watching the example you set.

- Don't fall for the latest theories with regard to human nature, cultural influences and alleged systemic injustices. Human nature doesn't care about any of that. Human nature has never changed and will never change, and therefore the fundamentals of effective leadership never change.

- The best leaders serve their people, always, in everything.

- Plan ahead a lot but be decisive and act now.

- Own your mistakes, privately and publicly. Never explain them away, even if you can.

- A great idea does not make a great business. Only great leadership can get you all of the necessary ingredients to make a great business.

- Communicate a lot; but only if what you're communicating is consistent, clear and concise.

- Lead people. Manage things.

- You can't make people care more than you do. You can inspire them in the hope that they will.

- Seeking agreement on outcomes is far more important than finding agreement on how to get there.

- There's no "your truth." Only *the* truth (sorry, *Oprah*). Embracing it saves a lot of time and effort.

- Praise in public; punish in private. And praise your people, a lot.

- Optimism and humor are far more effective than pessimism and bad temper.

- Laugh at yourself. Others will, so you might as well join in. Genuine humility is infectious.

- Culture eats strategy for breakfast (stolen from *Peter Drucker*).

- Protect your innovation all you want but remember that it's being copied already.

- The more you try to protect your intellectual property, the more others will try to take it.

- Don't be concerned with competitors. Make them be concerned with you.

- Encourage everyone to attain excellence. And never allow those who don't to set the standards.

- You're not really all that important. You're really not.

- Few things are ever as urgent as you think they are.

- Sleep on the big decisions. They can generally wait, and time almost always provides more clarity.

- Gaining trust as a leader takes years. Losing it takes seconds. And trust is everything.

- Reward those who show up, not those who suck up.

- Everything in life and in leadership is about balance. Work on the balance all the time.

My list could go on for far longer; and I'm certain you can add many more of your own. I encourage you to make a list of leadership truisms, and check things off from time to time. It's another truism that all good leaders need to be remined about the fundamentals of leadership.

Leadership & Finding Unity in Crisis

Human beings, we're told, are 99.9% identical, genetically. But that 0.1% sure creates a lot of strife among us, doesn't it? That math represents real opportunity, however, for effective leaders to bring people together in a time of crisis.

My wonderful Mother passed away this spring, and her rich legacy included being the "inventor" of the modern usage of the yellow ribbon. Her husband was Bruce Laingen who was the head of the U.S. Embassy in Iran during the hostage crisis there from 1979-1981. As the "senior spouse," she was thrust into a semi-official role as leader and spokesperson for the hostage families during an unprecedented time in our history. She balanced numerous constituencies, from State Department and DoD officials, to media contacts, to the many diverse spouses who looked to her for guidance and leadership in a stressful time.

In that role, Mom placed a simple yellow ribbon around the oak tree in her front yard in the D.C. suburbs, echoing the hopeful refrain from the Tony Orlando musical hit of the period. It was a simple act, just a piece of cloth around a single tree in an otherwise unknown neighborhood. But for those who knew her, Penne Laingen's seemingly simple decision was a deliberate act of leadership, as real and ultimately as powerful as President Carter's executive actions during that period. Thanks in part to her innate humanity, and coupled with hard lessons learned during often thankless service alongside her husband during challenging overseas postings over many years, she understood that leadership in that moment required patience, grace, and most of all a unifying symbol that exemplified the common purpose of the American people.

This was no easy task, frankly. President Carter was faced with a nearly impossible situation, with little military or diplomatic recourse to end the crisis on favorable terms; and

Americans were becoming divided and agitated, evidenced by the crisis' birthing of the 24/7 news cycle. Yet Penne Laingen had the self-awareness of effective leadership, fully appreciating that we have the vast genetic common ground of 99.9%; but also the realization that the differences in our lived experiences make that 0.1% difference vast and profound. The key for effective leadership is understanding that profundity and its roots that are very real for individuals, while drawing upon the abundance of compassion that ultimately makes up the human condition.

Today, we could use that level of leadership; leadership that seems as simple as tying a yellow ribbon around a tree and appealing for hope – yet was tied there with a purpose that comes from knowing that building unity of purpose takes looking past symbols and embracing and truly understanding the less than one percent of differences that normally explode those efforts.

Leaders who get that… leaders who fight for common purpose during the worst of times… leaders who truly understand what unifies… that's who we need in times of crisis. That's who we need right now.

Leadership & "Who You Know"

Even in the merit-based world of the military, where my professional career began, the saying *"It's not what you know, it's who you know"* becomes more relevant as one moves up in rank. This truism understandably frustrates fair-minded people. But I'm of the mind that human nature is a tough thing to change, and that there's another way to look at it. Perhaps it's better to ask: *"How do I become that person who others desire to know?"* I've known several people in my career who were "the person to know." They all achieved that status in different ways.

The first was not one person, but several great leaders I knew in the military and in business. They each lived by a simple doctrine: <u>immerse yourself in where you are, not where you're going</u>. Don't think of where you're at as the next ticket to punch to advance your career. Serve your organization and your people as if this was your final stop in the journey. Go all in for the here and now. They all lived that example, and I'm assuming they consciously modeled that in hopes that others would do the same.

The second example is a senior Army chaplain that I'm privileged to know. After leaving the military, I connected with him through volunteer service. I admire him immensely as a servant leader who inspires performance in people. I asked him once what he thought was the most important thing one can do for others, to advance their careers? His answer surprised me. It wasn't help them to know the right people, or encourage them to get a certain degree or certification. It was simply to teach and inspire them to <u>look for ways to express gratitude to others</u>; to give thanks for all manner of things, big and small, and to not expect anything in return.

Third, I learned from a good friend about her Father's approach to parenthood, and how he became "the person to know." He was a good father, and a good friend to others, she told me, not because he was especially, inherently good at parenting or being a friend; but rather because <u>he was always there</u> when she needed him, or when his friends needed him, for big things and small things. All things, and always. It's q*uantity* time, not quality time that matters, he had told her – the opposite of what generations of working parents have been told.

All of these leaders were effective for lots of reasons; but they became the "people to know" through their own unique outlooks on leadership. Pretty good ones, in my estimation. Finally, perhaps there's a different way to consider this phenomenon altogether: what's the end goal of wanting to know that one person, or to become that person? Is it strictly to get promoted, or to be able to promote people you know? What if, instead, the end goal was to simply be of service to others? Whatever that does for your own career, you'd certainly be someone people would want to know. And that's a pretty good career aspiration on its own.

Leadership & An Epilogue

After I wrote my first brief essay on leadership, it crossed my mind that I might write a few more. I didn't, however, think they would number 80 within just a few years. I now realize that it's an inexhaustible topic, as we both lead and are led by others in so many aspects of our lives. Add human nature, and all of a sudden there are infinite ways that leadership can achieve great things – or not; and ways we can be gratified in the process – or not. No wonder it's a topic that everyone has an opinion about, and one that seems to perpetually suggest yet another essay.

As I reflected on my own opinions that comprise these two 40-essay volumes, I wondered if there was a common overlay that is central to effective leadership… some aspect of human nature that doesn't lend itself to the way I segmented the topic over those 80 times. What came to mind was *authenticity*.

We can study about and improve upon ways to communicate, to signal empathy, to be decisive, to delegate, to listen better, and so many more skills and attributes. Attention to each of them can improve our leadership, certainly. But without a *genuine* care and concern for the mission and for its people, we're only making marginal improvements to mission effectiveness, and to the contentment of those being led. Human nature has a sixth sense for authenticity. People know it and appreciate it when they see it, and their judgment is harsh when they don't.

Being wholly authentic is hard, however. If we're honest, we don't *always* love the work we're responsible for, and we don't fully get along with *everyone* we lead (another reality of human nature). In my experience, there's a workaround for both of these realities. For the work at hand, it means not *needing* to love it, but rather needing to be immersed in it no matter how you feel about it. Like learning a language, full immersion leads to mastery, and mastery generally leads to great outcomes. And that's where the joy in the mission can ultimately be realized.

And what about the people you don't get along with? Immersion applies there as well. Get to know them and understand them fully, rather than trying to like them. As the political commentator Dennis Prager says, *"I prefer clarity over agreement."* And who knows – gaining that clarity may mean you end up liking them a little better, too.

Being genuine and authentic doesn't mean that you're going to get everything right, of course. But those being led can and will perceive the effort... and if you're getting most of the basics right (reference my 80 essays), they can forgive some human failings, after all.

Finally, I will say that practicing effective leadership, continuing to learn and improve, being a servant to those you lead, and being wholly genuine in the process can be – as it has been for me – enormously fun and ultimately deeply rewarding. Leadership at its core is influence. To influence individuals and teams to achieve great things, and celebrating in successes together has been one of the great joys of my life.

Leadership Matters

About the Author

Chip Laingen is the Executive Director of Defense Alliance, the Upper Midwest defense industry network, with members in 37 states. The Alliance was presented the prestigious "Progress Minnesota" award in 2014, became one of the nation's three Advanced Defense Technology Clusters in 2010 and won the Veterans Small Business Champion of the Year Award in 2007. He is on the Advisory Committee for Full Stack Saint Paul, Cyber Security Summit and Midwest Cleantech Open; and previously served on the executive commission of the Minnesota Science & Technology Authority, the AirSpace MN and Robotics Alley Advisory Committees, and was selected as an Executive Fellow for the University of Minnesota's Center for Integrative Leadership in 2012. In 2011 he joined the graduate faculty at the University of Minnesota's Technological Leadership Institute where he teaches Risk Communications and Policy for Security. He is a past President of the Twin Cities Council of the Navy League and is the author of "Laingen on Leadership."

Chip is also the Vice President, Midwest Region, Logistic Specialties, Inc. (LSI). He is an experienced professional for industry and technology-based business and economic development, with core expertise in Federal procurement, cluster development, and leadership development. In 2022, Chip was named the national Cybersecurity Summit's Visionary Academic Leader; included among the Notable Military Veteran Executives selected by the Twin Cities Business Magazine; and received the Peterson award from the National Contract Management Association for excellence in Federal government contract management.

Commander Laingen is a 21-year Veteran of the U.S. Navy. A 1983 graduate of the University of Minnesota NROTC, he earned a B.A. degree in International Relations. Designated a Naval Aviator in 1985, he was assigned to seagoing squadrons aboard aircraft carriers, cruisers, frigates and destroyers, amassing 3,000 fixed and rotary wing flight hours, including combat support flight time during Operations Desert Shield and Desert Storm in 1990-1991. He is also a qualified Officer of the Deck – Surface Warfare/Underway.

CDR Laingen was assigned to the NROTC Unit, University of Minnesota, where he served as Executive Officer/Associate Professor of Naval Science. He earned his M.A. in Public Affairs from the Humphrey School, and received the Student Leadership Award. He served as one of the two annual Admiral Arthur S. Moreau scholars for Ph.D. study in International Relations and Strategy at Tufts University's Fletcher School of Law and Diplomacy, earning the National Security subspecialty and Joint Professional Military Education codes. CDR Laingen was the Speechwriter to the Secretary of the Navy during the tenures of the 70th and 71st Secretaries.

His final tour was as the Executive and Commanding Officer of Helicopter Training Squadron Eight. During his tour as CO the squadron was named the number one advanced squadron among 17 in the naval air training command, and received the Chief of Naval Operations Aviation Safety Award and the Secretary of the Navy Safety Award, as the squadron surpassed 900,000 mishap free flight hours. He retired from active duty in September 2004.

CDR Laingen's awards include the Meritorious Service Medal with two Gold Stars, the Navy Commendation Medal with three Gold Stars and the Navy Achievement Medal with one Gold Star. He grew up in a Foreign Service family and lived in Pakistan, Afghanistan, Malta, and his hometown of Bethesda, Maryland.

www.ingramcontent.com/pod-product-compliance
Lightning Source LLC
Chambersburg PA
CBHW070754220526
45467CB00014B/408